I'M UP TO SOMETHING:

STEM MADE ME

BARTHOLOMEW PEREZ

NEW DEGREE PRESS

COPYRIGHT © 2021 BARTHOLOMEW PEREZ

I'M UP TO SOMETHING
STEM Made Me

ISBN   978-1-63730-662-8   *Paperback*

          978-1-63730-747-2   *Kindle Ebook*

          978-1-63730-936-0   *Ebook*

Epigraph

*I have said countless times, high performance people
are never satisfied with what they do or how they do
it! Hence, I am always endeavoring to improve."*

—DAN PEÑA

CONTENTS

———

NOTE FROM THE AUTHOR

———

If my life was a poker hand, then I was dealt a pair of fours, which was enough to convince myself I could play the hand and bluff my way into a win. Adversity was nonnegotiable as a first-generation, low-income person of color. Only after realizing I had the tools—education, mindset, and transferable skills—necessary to see my pair of fours as a winning hand did my situation evolve.

I'm up to something. I never knew what or how, but I knew I could achieve greater.

If there is anything I wish to accomplish with this book, it's to answer common questions and relieve doubts that first-generation persons might have by sharing experiences they may relate to and new ideas that may feed their curiosity. Nobody should have to fight their impostor syndrome alone. One achievement at a time is a prescription worthy for combating the petrifying effects of impostor syndrome.

Impostor syndrome is not a disease, but it is a feeling of persistent inadequacy despite ongoing successes. Dismissing events like passing a difficult exam, placing first in a competition, finishing undergrad, finishing graduate school, and receiving recognition at work, school, or in the community are all examples of successes we might achieve and still feel inadequate. Sound familiar? It does to me—all the time.

Before writing my memoir, one of the biggest external objections I faced was thinking, *But you are only twenty-nine.*

On November 16, 2021, I will be thirty. Going into my thirties, my pair of fours evolved into three fours. Now, I have the lens of science, technology, engineering, and mathematics (STEM) to clear my vision and the arts to enhance it. Leveraging STEM has allowed for a multicareer portfolio in engineering, real estate, writing, and investing.

The key ingredient was believing I could.

How? I leveraged my undergraduate skills in communication, critical thinking, marketing, sales, and networking. Proficiency in these domains is liberating, very much like switching out of sweat-drenched clothing after a high-intensity interval workout and putting on fresh gear. Feelings of liberation inspired me to write this book.

University's role in all of this was channeling these skills, but the real development happened throughout my youth, teens, and young adult life. This book is not meant to be a prescription but rather one of the many possibilities we first-generation, low socioeconomic persons can use to our benefit. My saving grace was a STEM education.

Echándole ganas has been my prerogative from my parents' decision to immigrate to the United States. At the very least, this meant finishing undergrad to begin establishing my version of wealth and giving back to the community that lifted me up. Pioneering is part of the first-generation story, and I was ready to embark on a life that was satisfying and engaging as the second scene in Lin-Manuel Miranda's *Hamilton* or a rerun of Bill Nye's *Bill Nye the Science Guy.*

Growing up was about survival. Survival meant receiving decent school grades, missing gang affiliations and crossfire, avoiding teenage pregnancy, swerving drugs, and developing my identity. Many of my peers fell victim to some or all of these events. I was fortunate and migrated away from the life limited by Little Armenia, Los Angeles, and into the rest of the world.

My biggest role model throughout my journey has been my mother. Her ability to balance work, raise three children, remain involved with us in school, and make time to help us with homework was super heroic. Compared to my mother's work ethic, I felt inadequate. I constantly pushed myself to work harder, thinking I should be able to balance school, a social life, community involvement, and fulfilling careers. Failure and shame were amplified by a need to become a jack of common trades and master of many.

Generally, Latinos thrive on being independent. Asking for help is seen as a weakness, and working rigorously is in our

DNA. We will work ourselves to death by working harder as opposed to smarter. At the core of my adversity was an understanding *I* was my biggest obstacle battling impostor syndrome. Impostor syndrome is managed daily, very much like flossing.

There was limiting self-talk of how I did not know enough, possess the right skills, or fit in. By the time I left home at seventeen, this was the mindset that had to evolve. In all my endeavors, I learned to leverage what I do and do not know from engineering to move forward and use my first-generation identity as a special power—the power of code-switching. Engineering milestones like the Technical Review Board, drafting an offer on a listing that has multiple offers, and negotiating favorable terms for a client are not very different when you can see the transferable skills—and I can do it all in English, Spanish, American Sign Language, or a mix of them all.

Growing up in Los Angeles was great because of its diversity. Evolving my experiences with different groups was important to navigate the corporate, entrepreneurial, and philanthropic realms. That meant dissolving the victim mentality and getting away from a belief all white people were rich, racist, and had no problems like first-generation people of color.

This belief had to come from my babysitter, television, and life. We did not have cable, so we were limited to regular programming, and whether it was on Univision, Telemundo, KTLA, or FOX, the majority of people on TV were fair-skinned and, in my mind, had to be white. My favorite characters were white. Subconsciously, I believed anyone with fair skin had it all; security, safety, money, and happiness—all things I wanted. There came a point I wished I was white, as I imagined life would be easier. I'd eventually learn white people are faced with their own set of battles.

My experience with white people was and continues to be confusing. While there were nice white people, there were also those who wanted to bring me harm.

I had to train myself to see beyond the discrimination whenever I questioned my position. No two situations are similar, but every experience helps navigate the next.

Only after reframing my perspective from "hard work" to "smart work" and looking at asking for help as a strength did I give myself permission to internalize my successes and challenge discrimination.

This battle against impostor syndrome begged the question, *How many other first-generation Latinos battle this phenomenon?*

"If the United States Latinos were considered their own country, it would be the seventh-largest economy in the world, making it bigger than any Latin American country, including Brazil and Mexico," which makes us a powerhouse (Guida, 2020). When we start talking about business, the common belief from the public (and Latinos) is we are too young or uneducated to pursue those ventures. If we are so young and uneducated, how do we explain "Latino employees entering the labor force offset declines from the outgoing baby boomers" (Salas, 2020)? Furthermore, "despite being only

18.3 percent of the US population, Latinos are responsible for 78 percent of the growth of the US labor force since the Great Recession" (Latino Donor Collaborative, 2020).

We are many, and we are mighty, but for many of us growing up, we did not have "role models who look like us, sound like us, or face the challenges we do. As Latinos, it's easy to downplay ourselves and attribute success to luck rather than hard work and focus" (Espriu, 2020). The unfortunate part of this story is many of us will continue to deny the feeling until we hear someone else has experienced this phenomenon.

Writing this book meant having the privilege to revisit childhood and teenage occurrences of trauma, confusion, relief, and pride that influenced my adult life as an engineer, realtor, investor, and author.

I am sitting in Kona Coffee & Tea in Kailua-Kona, Hawaii, thinking, *How did I, Bartholomew Perez, get here?* By plane, of course, but I am dumbfounded by the reality I was there in Hawaii, writing. This is not the impostor syndrome taking the stage. This is gratitude taking the leading role.

I believe many of us don't need advice to get to where we want to go. We just need to know we are not alone. There is comfort and power in knowing another first-generation Latino born to immigrant parents of low socioeconomic status has achieved greatness. Not knowing we can do this makes us feel like pioneers, which is levels more intimidating and a recipe for anxiety. This was true for me. There have been instances in my engineering world where I was the diversity in the room and instances in my real estate world where my clients were levels more affluent and wealthier than I.

My high school teachers were right about one thing: university will reinforce the way we think. I am a first-generation, multicareer, college graduate with a bachelor's in mechanical engineering and a master's in Architecture-based Enterprise Systems Engineering, leading careers as a systems architect engineer at a Fortune 100 defense company, a realtor at one of the world's most innovative publicly traded cloud-based brokerages, and the author of *I'm up to Something: STEM Made Me.*

Everything sounds great now, but it was only after realizing my pair of fours afforded me the belief my hand could be a winning hand.

STAGE ONE

FIRST-GENERATION THINGS

CHAPTER 1.62

SLAPPED INTO CONSCIOUSNESS

———

I was only five, but my mind was older
My childhood was not extravagant, but I had family

My mom continues to believe I was too young
I understood more than she thinks

Seeing parents fight would wake anybody
I've been woke since

My experiences influence the type of family I want one day
My vision has never been clearer

———

Three hours north from the city of Oaxaca, high into the summits that could only be reached via a shuttle only meant for four people stuffing seven in, is where my journey begins. Oaxaca is a state in southern Mexico, rich in natural resources and known for its large Indigenous population. It has roots in the Aztec, Mixtec, and Zapotec civilizations, all of which were native to this region and whose influence remains alive to this day. My parents' independent decisions to leave their Headquarters gave me, Bartholomew Perez, life.

I am a first-generation Mexican American born into low socioeconomic status in *los Estados Unidos*. Being born in *los Estados Unidos* afforded me the possibility to evolve into a multicareer professional navigating the intricacies of my Headquarters in California as an engineer, real estate professional, and author. I didn't know this growing up, but the bits and pieces of these manifestations were always there.

Throughout my life, Headquarters were the different places I considered home. Headquarters were not limited to where I lived. It also expanded to where I felt welcomed, safe, most connected, and expected to give maximum effort for my greater good. Yes, this definition is generic, but so are sayings like:

- Home is where the heart is.
- Home is a structure sustained by love.
- Home is where families are made, and memories are created.

Headquarters is where I was unknowingly up to something. That something would evolve into a future I didn't know existed for someone like me—poor, first-generation, and Mexican. My collection of experiences would build a narrative to one day talk about the premise STEM taught me to see beyond my circumstance and appreciate the tools and experiences essential to lifting me up. Before I could enter my Headquarters, my parents had to leave theirs.

My parents grew up in different villages way up in the mountains where electricity was a luxury, machines were few, roads were without pavement, agriculture was the primary source of earning a living, and life was the epitome of simplicity. Both my mom and dad were of humble Indigenous backgrounds.

Clara, *mi mamá*, had a brief college education and was an aspiring teacher. Her father paid for her schooling with the money he earned from harvesting coffee from the fields he owned. This was an extremely laborious process he took complete responsibility for from start to finish, just as the three generations before him did. Harvesting included planting the coffee, picking the cherries, processing the cherries, drying the beans, milling the beans, grinding the beans, packaging the ground beans, and selling the coffee to the local villagers and the Oaxaca city folk.

The same way the fertilized soil nurtured those coffee beans, those same coffee beans nurtured my mom with tenacity for an unmatched work ethic from the labor required to make coffee.

Education was important for my mom, which is why she left her family for *los Estados Unidos* with the intent of collecting enough money to return to Mexico and finish her education. The price for tuition placed a heavy burden on their household. Although she was grateful, she knew she wanted to help her parents by helping offset costs with earnings she could bring from *los Estados Unidos* in a two-year period.

Rene, *mi papá*, had a third-grade education and dedicated himself to laboring on the sugarcane, agave, and coffee fields. He was hardworking and did not know much beyond manual labor. He decided to come to *los Estados Unidos* for a more comfortable future, where earnings might be higher. Dreams and aspirations for something greater were not a part of his long-term plan. He simply wanted to be. For my dad, as long as he was with family, he was satisfied. When his family members decided to come, he went with them. My dad was loved and taken care of as the youngest of eleven siblings.

Life in Oaxaca revolved around agriculture, and both my parents spoke the dialects of the native Zapotec people, which they preserved coming to *los Estados Unidos*. It is a language I never learned but knew enough from context to know when it was time to leave from visiting a relative, when I was in trouble, or when it was time to eat. The sound of Zapotec is as familiar as a *tlayuda con chorizo, quesillo, y chapulines.*

El sabor de Oaxaca es único.

My mom arrived in *los Estados Unidos* in October 1989. She would celebrate her first Christmas with her *primas* at the only place that was open after a long day of work at ten at night on Christmas—McDonald's on Vermont and Washington in Los Angeles. She did not have much, but she had family. She held several titles in those early years: waitress, seamstress, nanny, factory worker, and housekeeper—the latter is a role she maintains to this day.

My dad arrived sometime in 1989 and held many labor-intensive jobs in those early years in construction, dishwashing, and factory working. His calling was in the restaurant, washing dishes—which is a role he maintains to this day.

Soy el orgulloso hijo de housekeeper y lavaplatos.

Advancing, according to my parents, meant obtaining an education beyond high school to have a shot at something other than housekeeping and dishwashing. All I knew was there was an opportunity to do something different, and education was supposed to make that happen.

There is nothing wrong with washing dishes or housekeeping. In fact, whenever I clean and wash dishes, it is a reminder of the love and sacrifice from my parents. Nowhere in my vision was science, technology, engineering, and mathematics (STEM) a foreseeable professional option.

¿STEM? ¿Que es eso?

Before they were Mom and Dad, they were two strangers living in the same apartment building in Korea Town, Los Angeles. My dad pursued my mom relentlessly, not willing to take no for an answer. This is such a strange thought because my dad is a man of few words, so imagining him shooting his shot takes a lot of imagination.

I feel I should mention here—I was not supposed to happen.

My mom came to *los Estados Unidos* with a mission: *save enough money to return to Oaxaca, finish her education, and become a teacher.* After she became pregnant with me, her course changed, and she began to consider what living in *los Estados Unidos* might mean for my future. She knew the difficulty of living in Oaxaca and working the fields only to earn close to nothing, living in the village, and going to school in the city after hours on foot.

She also knew the difficulty of living *indocumentado* with a lack of opportunities or a voice. *Viviendo en los Estados Unidos como ciudadano* meant her son might have opportunities that would otherwise not exist in Oaxaca. It meant she did not want *her* struggles to become *my* struggles.

Gracias, mamá.

So, my parents decided to stay because abortion was not an option for my Catholic mom. She once told me she was nearly convinced into becoming a nun. Had she, I would not have happened.

Thank you, Mom.

Following their decision to stay, they had two more children, Rene and Gabriel, born in December 1992 and August 1995, respectively. Being close in age was great. We held plenty of similar interests, plenty to fight about, and plenty to dream up and make-believe. My parents made it clear as long as we were in their Headquarters, the expectation was for us to finish high school. Opportunities were never straightforward—they never are—but my mom tried to make use of what she could.

An example is Medi-Cal. This is one of the many programs low socioeconomic persons should be aware of but are often not. When I was young, I faced a fever of 104 degrees Fahrenheit where *remedios* were not enough.

Visiting the doctor *era caro*. That doctor's visit cost my mom nearly a thousand dollars. This set her into tears because she had two other children to care for, and this was two months' worth of rent. Had it not been for one of the nurses at the clinic telling my mom to enroll us into Medi-Cal, we may not have received any much-needed future medical care or maintained medical records that would prove to be necessary for my mom to prove rights for custody.

Gracias, Medi-Cal.

The same goes for the Special Supplemental Nutrition Program for Women, Infants, and Children (WIC). Yes, I was a WIC baby, and this relieved a huge burden for my parents. Because of WIC, we had bread, milk, cereal, cheese, yogurt, oats, and Welch's juices in our fridge. I remember going to the WIC center and crossing my fingers that this time we would get Frosted Flakes or Lucky Charms, but it was always plain-old Kix and Chex.

Same way we had Medi-Cal and WIC for our daily lives, we had support for schooling. My mom was our advocate for education and was much more familiar with the benefits of being low-income within the Los Angeles Unified School District (LAUSD).

All my siblings and I knew graduating from twelfth grade was nonnegotiable. Being a part of LAUSD meant we had plenty of low-income programs for us to benefit from without really knowing about them: meals, libraries, computers, afterschool programs, field trips, and a playground. The benefit of the public school system was it was available to us so long as we lived nearby.

Yellow lunch tickets came in clutch when it was time to eat. These were playground currency. Sometimes, we would trade those tickets for Hot Cheetos or Doritos.

My parents spent most of their days working. When there was no nanny, we were the babysitters. Mom would wake up as early as two in the morning, alongside my dad, to prepare meals and mentally prepare themselves over *café y pan dulce*. We lived in a three-hundred-twenty-five-square-foot studio, which was really two hundred square feet because my parents pilled boxes on top of boxes like it was an Amazon warehouse.

I remember waking up to see my dad leave at three in the morning, and if he left any later, he would miss the bus that would take him straight into Downtown Los Angeles, where his factory job was waiting for him.

The factory he worked at produced, packaged, and sold fishcakes of all kinds. My dad's role was to prepare the machines for production and packaging. The work required lifting heavy metal containers, large quantities of boxes, and moving of foodstuffs that were going into a machine to grind and purée the fishcakes. It was repetitive, physically demanding, and there were no breaks.

I saw how difficult the job could be firsthand.

I am unsure what compelled me to join my dad—maybe it was my parents' idea. My first time inside a factory was at age eight. I was thinking about all the money I was going to make from a day's worth of work. The minimum wage at the time was five dollars and twenty-five cents an hour, and my expectation for eight hours' worth of work was forty-two dollars.

My take-home pay was twenty dollars—the most meaningful twenty dollars I ever earned.

Twenty was not forty-two, but I was happy with my earnings. I wanted to go back, but my dad would not allow it. My parents feared if I started seeing money too young, I would forget about school. Many of my early childhood friends, who were also first-generation, expressed their parents held a similar fear. It makes sense since their motive for leaving their Headquarters was the money.

I was proud of the time I spent working with my dad. It felt like I was contributing to making work a bit easier for him, but I probably made him more anxious by being there. After all, there were large industrial machines that could have eaten me up like a shredder consuming paper.

That said, there was plenty I did not like about the job.

It was a very loud environment, with all the machines running at the same time—much like an orchestra with no conductor. They dedicated hardly any time to breaks because shipments had to be packed and sent out to customers. Everyone seemed to be in a hurry while the supervisors were perching out of the office overhead to oversee the operations.

There was also a horror story of one of my father's coworkers whose hand was caught in the machine, resulting in him having to receive surgery to salvage the body part. The procedure was a success, but the functionality of his hand was not the same. I did not want to lose any body parts. I enjoyed playing video games, sports, and going to school too much.

It also paid minimum wage.

This was probably the real motive for having me join my father: the lesson that there are far better jobs that could pay better than minimum wage and be less physically demanding. By the end of this experience, I did not want a factory job.

After my father left for work, my mom stayed up to prepare meals for the day, making sure we had something to eat for dinner. Once my mom dropped us off at school, she made her way by bus to the large houses in Beverly Hills, Culver City, and Santa Monica that would often appear on television. While I never joined her for work, she would tell us she did not want us *limpiando baños para ganar dinero*—cleaning bathrooms was the last thing she wanted for our future.

Knowing what I know today about square footage in these homes, I know there was too much space for one person to clean on their own. They exploited my mom, but she did not see it that way. She saw it as an opportunity to earn a living. There are days when I feel my mom's hands and they are as rough as sandpaper from all the chemicals she used to clean those homes. Anything that feels like sandpaper shatters me because it reminds me of her.

"Hijo, no quiero esta vida para ustedes. Estudia y termina tus estudios" would be the words my mom would tell us before we left for school.

I never understood why my parents felt they had to do these jobs. Yes, they were *indocumentados*, but why settle? I came to learn citizenship in the late 1980s and early 1990s was possible for about five hundred dollars, but they passed up on the opportunities because it required money they did not have or want to borrow. When they arrived, the minimum wage was about three dollars an hour.

Ser ciudadano would have meant being able to apply for jobs, receive government assistance, schooling, traveling anxiety-free, and being able to move forward for themselves. These are all the benefits I, as a first-generation United States citizen, have had.

I was a really good student, obedient for the most part, always minding my own business in elementary and high school. I stayed in school because of the work my parents did, worrying my fate would be similar to theirs if I opted out of school—cleaning houses, scrubbing toilets, or working in a factory.

Mom took care of the majority of our upbringing. She cooked, cleaned, helped us with our homework, and made sure we were healthy. Meanwhile, Dad would be out with his family, drinking and going to local recreation centers to play basketball and participate in tournaments. My dad facilitated the socialization, as we would see our cousins on his side of the family regularly.

My parents were *old-school Latinos* in the sense they believed in *nalgadas*. There was an art behind *nalgadas*, whether it was a belt, hanger, cables, the palms of their hands, wooden spoons, or the infamous *chancla*.

Discipline was in order when we talked back, didn't follow the rules, were obnoxious, roughhoused, or were disrespectful. Our Headquarters was all boys, and there was a lot of rough behavior. In the two hundred square feet of space we had, there was only so much we could do with six of us living there.

Cramped is an understatement with two hundred square feet of space for both my parents, siblings, and uncle. *Tío Mundo* was the fun uncle who made sure we were entertained when my parents were away. The WWE, NBA, and *barajas* were how we bonded with *Tío Mundo*. He worked construction and did not have a family of his own. Between him and my mom, they stuck together after leaving Oaxaca.

My dad and uncle never spoke, but they managed to live under the same roof. How this was possible is a mystery to me.

I never quite understood my parents' relationship. There was a lot of fighting in the early years. A majority of these fights revolved around my dad spending a lot of his time away from home and coming home drunk well into the next day. With the alcohol came infidelity, and I even witnessed some of it.

There were days I would go to my cousins' house with my dad, and he would go out to the local nightclub. On several occasions, I remember crying to try to keep him from leaving.

Things got so bad in our home my mom changed the locks on the door to keep him out. Of course, he found out when his keys did not work. On one of the days this happened, instead of just leaving for his sister's home, my dad made his way in through an open window on the first floor and started yelling at my mom.

The yelling escalated in our two-hundred-square-foot studio, and suddenly, our apartment looked more like a boxing ring.

This is one of my most vivid memories from my childhood, and this is how I was figuratively slapped into consciousness. No harm came to my siblings and I, but it was the fear, confusion, crying, and anxiety that left its mark. I was no older than five because my baby brother, Gabriel, was a newborn, and I remember him being wrapped in the white baby blanket he came with from the hospital.

What began as a verbal exchange escalated into physical. My dad hit my mom in the face with the back of his hand. My mom was four-foot-eleven and my dad five-foot-three and about forty pounds heavier. Despite the numbers, my mom fought back. The few decorations and belongings we had crashed down. I remember a transparent corded telephone connected to a landline that lay on the ground beeping at what felt like a rate faster than light with no end. My brothers and I were sitting on a little twin-sized mattress, holding onto one another, not knowing what to do.

As soon as it started, it was over.

My baby brother was crying hysterically.

My dad left, and my mom had to force herself back up and act as if nothing had happened. This is the extent of the memory, but it was enough to begin the stream of childhood memories I have.

Growing up, the most important aspect of my childhood was having my siblings. Going into my adult life, I realized this made the biggest difference in my development. Fighting each other, strangely enough, brought us closer and made me resilient to the different worlds I now navigate. I love my mom for doing everything she could and stopping at nothing to provide the best she could. I love my dad for sticking around and participating the best he could.

Although it is not an excuse, they were young parents and did not plan for any of what happened to them or the family they built.

These experiences helped me realize the sort of family I would one day want for myself.

GOTTA CATCH 'EM ALL

———

My fascination with Pokémon was about escaping reality
I felt like I lived inside a Poké Ball

I was not allowed to adventure
So I adventured with imagination

Entrepreneurship was an unfamiliar concept
At age eight, this meant selling toys and Pokémon cards

I was proud to make sales and cash flow
Making money at eight was about helping my mother

Early business lessons compounded into my adult life
I definitely felt like I caught them all

———

Cassettes, CD players, dial-up internet, and slime were some of the technological breakthroughs of the 1990s. Okay, slime was not really a breakthrough, but it was a big deal. There was a segment on cable TV dedicated to sliming celebrities with buckets of slime. We did not have cable TV, so I only heard about this from the schoolkids.

The internet was far too slow to depend on dial-up to stream. There were times you would wait through buffering only to be forced to refresh the page.

I remember the nineties being a time when computers, the internet, and cellphones were becoming more available. We did not yet own or operate any of these in our Headquarters, but we would regularly go to the local public library so we could use computers and the internet. Most of our time on the computer was spent on the internet playing games or a Word document typing a school assignment or googling all the foods we wanted to eat.

Browsing through pictures of food was a thing for my siblings and me—fast food anyway, because we rarely ate at restaurants, with Clifton's Cafeteria in DTLA as an exception. McDonald's and Burger King were conveniently down the street.

Going to the library meant we were surrounded by books, but my siblings and I were not readers. My mom tried really hard to encourage us to read. We would check out dozens of books at a time, filling a rolling Pokémon backpack for us to take back to Headquarters with us. Sometimes we would fill two backpacks. These backpacks would go untouched if it wasn't for our school reading logs. School reading logs were designed to hold us accountable and ensure we were able to sustain a proficient to advanced reading level. The more we read, the more we were rewarded in the form of raffle tickets.

Raffle tickets sustained my motivation to maintain a proficient reading level. Being an English as a Second Language (ESL) student came with its own set of challenges.

Being an ESL student meant there would be a lot of words that were my enemies. Writing was the worst, including remembering things like "-i before -e, except after -c." Like, why? Then there were words that were spelled completely different from how they sounded.

Books were kicked to the side when television was our primary form of entertainment, which had the added benefit of working as our babysitter. We glued ourselves to the screen, which is probably why we developed a need for glasses. Obviously, our astigmatism had nothing to do with our poor vision.

Saturday mornings, we dedicated to new episodes of our favorite cartoons. Smartphones and streaming were not a thing. We had to wait for our dose of cartoons and could never agree about which shows to watch. The biggest dispute was between Pokémon and Digimon. They were both on at the same time, and having one television meant we would create a ruckus over which we were going to watch.

Being the eldest, it was easy to have my way. To settle the dispute, we would wrestle like it was the WWE. The disputes would not last long, and someone would break up the fights before any of us could get hurt. To have some democracy, the decision was made based on what show we watched the last time. This was before we knew what democracy even was.

In Pikachu we trusted.

Before the Pokémon TV series came the Game Boy *Pokémon Red Version* and *Pokémon Blue Version*, where we could all participate in catching all 151 Pokémon. I remember us only having one turquoise Game Boy Color console and having to share. Three of anything was expensive in our Headquarters, but for my parents' sanity, it made sense for each one of us to have our own console. When we did, we would spend hours training and collecting our Pokémon.

The craze between the Game Boy and TV series drew us to the trading card game. This phenomenon swept our entire school.

The card game was one of the most popular subjects on the playground. Like any good citizen at Santa Monica Boulevard Elementary School, I had to take part. By now, we had been very well acquainted with the TV series and video games, so logically, we had to start collecting cards.

Those 2.48-inch-by-3.46-inch cards caused a lot of anticipation among children and growing concern among parents. I knew it, too, because my mom would sometimes refer to them as *mugrosos* Pokémon when we would be consumed by them.

Parents were urged not to let their children play, collect, or buy Pokémon cards because of the message of violence, which allegedly turned the playground into a black market. We, the schoolkids at Santa Monica, saw Pokémon as the one thing that brought us together. My mom learned to make the card collecting an incentive for completing chores, doing well on exams, and helping each other in our schoolwork—anything for a booster pack!

Opening booster packs was the equivalent of playing scratchers or blackjack. You would win or you would lose—mostly lose—and still go back because this time, it was going to be different. It was only five dollars per pack, but five dollars added up quickly between the three of us. Sometimes, though, five dollars was totally worth it because we would pull a holographic first edition card from a booster.

We saved our favorites for being powerful, rare, and cool. Those cards included Charizard, Blastoise, Venusaur, Mewtwo, and Gyarados, and we kept them in a separate binder for safekeeping.

At the time, these cards might have had a resale value of a few hundred dollars, so building on our collection meant we had to actively trade, play for keeps, or wait until we could buy more. This was how I discovered an acumen for business, sales, and entrepreneurship before I could even spell "entrepreneurship."

Without realizing it, we were regularly appraising the value of these cards. We would follow up with calculating risk and potential return on investment when playing against the other kids, acknowledging their strengths and weaknesses while considering the opportunities and threats (SWOT) on the playground.

Eventually, we had a lot of repeat cards and noticed some kids were willing to buy them to complete their own collections. We did not need Amazon or eBay to tell us there was value here because we would hear about it from the consumers.

As the young entrepreneurs we were, we needed to find a way to accurately appraise the near-true value of what we had before setting or accepting an offer. We regularly visited GameStop because they had catalogs with prices on what these cards were worth. There were new catalog issues every month, and we would purchase them to reevaluate what we had.

Our favorite cards were also everyone else's favorites, and we would not risk losing them or having them stolen. We kept these in a different binder at Headquarters in penny sleeves and top loaders because we would hear stories of kids getting jumped for their cards. This was also a great lesson on letting people know how much you really have. *Envidia y maldad* were usually the result of the other schoolkids knowing too much—*todo por presumir.*

This was where the parents' concerns came from because fights would break out as soon as someone tried to steal cards.

As an adult, looking back, the idea of selling our cards went deeper than just wanting to make money or having a complete collection of all 151 Pokémon at the time. The deeper motive came from the thought we could potentially relieve some of the financial burdens from my mom so she could spend more time with us. She would wake up crazy early to prepare our meals, go to work, and make it home in time to help us with our homework.

I was only eight and already up to something. My Big, Hairy, Audacious Goal (BHAG) evolved into trying to earn enough money, so my mom did not have to work anymore. My mom did most of the parenting and was heavily involved with our schooling to make sure we were performing the best we could in those early years.

Having us succeed in school meant she was also fulfilling her own childhood dreams of receiving an education and evolving beyond the coffee fields she grew up in.

I was always baffled by my mom's time management. She made time to attend our parent-teacher meetings and back-to-school nights while being enrolled in night classes to learn English and getting up early to do it all over again. I understand the sacrifices she made. My mom never complained about life being unfair. It was from her example of tenacity, time management, work ethic, and nurture I get my strength from today.

Lack of money or time would not be an excuse.

Yes, we lived in a two-parent household, but my dad was just physically there most of the time. He would pick us up from school, occasionally take us out, and make sure we ate the dinner Mom prepared, but he was a very quiet and serious man. He did not show affection or speak much. We learned to associate him being physically present as his way of showing he loved us.

In my mind, the dads were supposed to work, which was why I did not consider him in my BHAG.

To get anywhere near our BHAG, we had to scale our trading and selling. This was how Ricky became our associate. Ricky had been in my first-, second-, and third-grade classes, so we were buddies but not best friends. We had a mutual friend, Hessler, which was probably why this partnership made sense to me.

Hessler and I had similar interests in sports, math, and science, and we were competitive. What I liked about Ricky was he was very social, well-mannered, and all the girls liked him because he was polite. There was never a time Ricky seemed threatening or capable of hurting someone. These qualities put me at ease. He also had a different group of friends than me, which could mean more customers, so with this eight-year-old rationality, we teamed up.

Before we sold cards, we tested the market by selling toys we no longer played with. Those Happy Meal McDonald's toys we had an endless supply of were a big part of our product. For eight-year-olds, our partnership was complex and being the ring leader, I suggested I should earn 25 percent commission from his sales. There were a lot of coins involved, so my mom bought each of my siblings and I a piggy bank. There was a Rottweiler, a Virgin Mary, and a pig made of ceramic. These would not last more than a month before we cracked them open because we would trade in our coins at the local Coinstar inside the Food 4 Less on Sunset and Western. More coins meant more cards.

Collecting a commission at age eight was important, and I was proud of this because we built it from innocent thoughts. I later learned my younger siblings were entrepreneurs in their own classrooms when they were roughly the same age. Rene was selling stationery, and Gabriel sold candy. When we talked about it as adults, we realized that it was all based on observation of what the other kids wanted and then feeding that demand. We had no formal training or anybody telling us that would be a good idea. We just did it.

Come to think of it, we also had a supply chain, an enterprise, operating procedures, market projections, and sales! That little eight-year-old entrepreneur was up to something all right. There was nothing to be shy about because I did not know any better. Fear and *vergüenza* of putting myself out there was not yet a thing. I was certain there were plenty of kids who wanted to buy cards and money to be made to help my mom.

Ricky and I became much better friends through our affiliation—until the time came when he tested our friendship.

"Can I borrow your collection to take home? I want to make a new plan for us," Ricky asked one day. I thought this was a strange request, but I was too naive to think he would not bring them back. Working with Ricky had helped me trust him.

"Yeah, sure! Just bring them back tomorrow," I stated.

"Of course, I promise."

I handed Ricky *my entire collection,* including those cards we had set aside as our prized cards. Tomorrow came and went, and so did the next day. I expected Ricky to hand me back my binders in the same condition I had handed them to him. When he didn't, I confronted him, and he was puzzled by my request.

"Ricky, where are my cards?" I asked, trembling.

"My cousin has them, and I am not sure when I will get them back," he said.

"You promised to bring them back tomorrow, and tomorrow passed three days ago."

"I know, but my cousin has them. Sorry."

This shattered me like a chandelier coming undone from a thirty-foot ceiling and crashing onto a hardwood floor. I knew my cards were gone forever. I should have seen this coming, but I was too trusting to think Ricky was capable of doing something like this.

We had several first edition and limited edition holographic cards that, in today's world, are difficult to come by. Now, if a single card was graded at Professional Sports Authenticator (PSA) as Grade Ten, it could easily be worth a few thousand dollars. The rarest of them all, Charizard, could go upward of fifty-five thousand dollars in pristine first edition condition. Yes, a single Pokémon card—which we had—could be a down payment toward homeownership in California in 2021.

It was a devastating experience, an important business lesson I could learn: never fully trust somebody just because they say they are your friend. With the right motivation, they can turn on you. This was also something I solemnly follow from Biggie's "Ten Crack Commandments."

I was left with so many questions. Did Ricky become my friend so he could steal my cards? Did I know his cousin, and did he go to Santa Monica Boulevard? Why go through all that trouble for cards? How was I going to help my mom? Today, I have to thank Ricky and his cousin for this painful but very necessary lesson that shaped me into the business professional I am today.

My third-grade teacher, Mrs. Smith, found me crying with my head down on my desk. I was not participating or completing any of my assignments, and she had the teaching assistant ask me what was wrong. I remember not wanting to talk. Eventually, I wrote what was happening on a piece of paper: "My Pokémon cards were stolen by Ricky." From this note, Mrs. Smith organized a parent-teacher conference so we could confront the situation. She did not have to do this, but she cared enough to try and settle this fairly.

It was an entire day before we had the parent-teacher conference. I spent the majority of the day crying. Explaining this to my siblings was difficult because I had no real reason other than Ricky being my friend. There was a sense of *vergüenza* in willingly handing the collection to him. Just like that, the idea of being able to help my mom was gone with that collection.

Recovering any part of the collection was not very realistic, but I hoped the parent-teacher conference would at least result in having some of the cards back. Moments before the meeting, it was awkward. A very strong sense of hate consumed me. This hate was toward myself, for being so trusting, and toward Ricky, for what felt like a setup. The betrayal hurt me.

Our conference began with an explanation of how Ricky stole the cards. No one used force or aggression to get the cards away from me. I willingly handed my collection over to Ricky based solely on the promise he would bring them back the next day. I almost wished I had been jumped instead because at least then I had a legit reason for losing my cards. Ricky explained how his cousin took the cards from him and had no way of getting them back.

After the explanation, Mrs. Smith proceeded to ask how much the collection was worth. At the time, I knew some of the cards could be worth hundreds if they were rated from a reputable source like PSA, but we only went based on the GameStop catalogs. I knew of the idea of hundreds of dollars but had never seen or held a denomination larger than a twenty-dollar bill.

The collection was worth a few thousand dollars. The day leading up to the meeting, I did not expect to be asked how much it was all worth during this conference. This caught me off guard.

I must have thought by stating its true value, they would not believe me, and there would not be an agreement. The first thing that came out of my mouth was "one hundred dollars."

In my current estimate, based on the mint condition of many cards, the first edition status, and probably having shadowless cards, the collection was easily worth fifty thousand, at a minimum, by 2021 standards.

"So the collection was worth a hundred dollars? Are you sure?" Mrs. Smith asked.

"I am sure."

Mrs. Smith turned to Ricky. "Very well. Please bring a hundred dollars to cover the cost of the cards that were stolen."

A one-hundred-dollar bill was, in my mind, the largest denomination possible. The collection was immensely undervalued, and I did not even recover half of what it was worth.

I avoid feelings of devastation and betrayal by properly appraising every situation I find myself in. It is for the best that lesson came as a child rather than as an adult. Ricky had his own agenda, and he was up to something.

That settled the case, and Ricky's mother would pay the one hundred dollars. With the money, Ricky gave me back some of the cards, I guess to maintain good faith with me. They were all commons and none of the valuable ones, of course. We never spoke again, and I avoided him.

Just like that, whatever first prospective business I set up was shut down. I have since learned not to mix business with pleasure and to never fully trust anybody but myself.

FOSTER CARE

———

Being forcefully removed changed me
The time we were gone felt like an eternity

My family was torn
My mom was not sure if she could retain custody

After it happened, my parents never spoke about the events
My siblings and I lived with our slice of trauma

It happened so suddenly, and there was no going back
Coming full circle with the events, there were no answers

———

Tetherball was one of the few sports I excelled at since I was small. I had the physics figured out. It was sometime during my fourth-grade year the tetherball poles were installed on our playground, and I played as much as I could during our recess and lunch. What I probably enjoyed the most was it was a solo sport. Cooperative play was important, but I did not like letting the team down for soccer, basketball, or kickball.

There were days we were allowed to stay after school to get some extra playtime, and on that particular day, I was getting more wins than usual. I was the self-proclaimed tetherball champion at Santa Monica Boulevard Elementary School.

The day began like any other. We woke up early, went to school, and enjoyed the history, math, and science lessons of the day. August 2000 seemed like any other time of year—until it wasn't. We remained on the playground for much longer during our physical education hour. I remember being on the tetherball court until the game was paused. My playmate stopped midgame and pointed behind me with a head nod. To both our surprise, it was the school nurse. She never left the office unless something was wrong.

"I am looking for Bartholomew Perez. Is that you?" she asked.

"Yes, that's me," I responded.

"Can you get your things and come with me, please?"

"What? Why?"

"I'll explain once we are in my office."

"Okay…"

"Is your brother, Rene, here too?"

"He should be in class right now in one of the bungalows." Clearly, something was wrong. I ran through a list of possible reasons why I would be summoned. I did not have lice or chicken pox, nor was I expecting any new vaccinations.

We left the tetherball court and made our way back to the school. There was a deafening silence that was filled by a breeze of anxiety that seemed to warn me a storm of devastation was coming to sweep me away. The walk to her office felt miles long.

Upon entering the nurse's office, I saw my baby brother, Gabriel. He looked sad. Not in tears, but I could tell he was hurt from his body language that was similar to Eeyore's. The nurse asked that I sit across from Gabriel. She asked him to roll up his pant sleeve to show me his right leg and then both of his arms.

"Did you do this to your brother?" the school nurse asked.

"Do what? The bug bites?" I asked, confused.

"Did you burn your brother?"

"Burn him? No. Where was he burned?"

She pointed to the round welts all over his leg. These marks were actually all over his body and ours. Mosquitoes showed no mercy during the summer. Since we had no central AC or a window unit, we would leave the windows open during the day and night. Not having window screens meant we were regularly breakfast, lunch, and dinner for mosquitoes.

If mosquitoes held a congregation anywhere in Los Angeles, it felt like our Headquarters was it. Blood was only one thing those mosquitoes would take from us. Any ounce of normalcy in our family was gone after this. As much as I explained, though, the nurse was convinced there was something else going on here.

"Your brother claims you burned him with cigarettes."

"I don't even smoke. Those are bug bites."

Gabriel got bit the worst out of all of us. We would tease that the mosquitoes picked him because they liked young blood from the chubby kids. Despite all the alcohol and hydrogen peroxide we used to treat the welts, he would constantly scratch. All the scratching caused scarring, which ranged from very round to very oval. Although not as bad, I had some of these bites too.

After the school nurse questioned me, she summoned Rene into her office. Once summoned, she asked Rene the same thing. To no surprise, he gave the same response as I did because it was the truth!

She examined all of us and noticed we had the same round welts all over our bodies. She must have been greatly concerned about the bug bites because the next thing we knew, there were two police officers in the nurse's office.

All this for mosquito bites!

"Does anybody in your family smoke cigarettes?" one of the officers asked.

"My parents don't smoke," I responded, not knowing my dad actually had a smoking habit. My mom was adamant he did not expose us, so he kept it a secret. It was a darn good secret because he never smelled like cigarette smoke.

"Where did these marks on your bodies come from? Did someone hurt you?"

"They are bug bites. My mom tells us not to scratch, but they get so itchy."

The bell rang for us to leave school and go to Headquarters, except that day, we were not going back. We were kept in the nurse's office while the police interrogated my dad. After thirty minutes of questioning, he was in handcuffs.

When one of the police officers asked him for identification, he lied about not having any on him. When they searched him and found he had his wallet and ID, they arrested him for lying. With his wallet, they also found a box of cigarettes, which made it all seem that much more suspicious. They must have thought, *What else is he hiding?*

From the nurse's office, we were escorted to the front of the school and placed into two separate police cars. One was for the three of us and the other for our dad. That was the first time we sat in the back of a police car. The seats were cold, hard plastic. There were no seatbelts, and there was a barrier between the officers and us.

We rarely found ourselves in any vehicles because my parents did not drive. Unless it was a taxi, we did not get into vehicles that were not a bus or train. Being in the back of a car was just as memorable as being inside a police car.

Before we arrived at the Hollywood Police Station on Fountain and Wilcox, we made a stop at McDonald's for Happy Meals. It was a fair attempt to get our minds away from what was going on. This must have been a gesture to get us to relax and talk, except there was really not much to say over bug bites.

At the time, there was no real way of knowing what prompted Gabriel to say we burned him. Yes, there was a lot of roughhousing at Headquarters, and with all the energy and testosterone of three growing boys, no neglect came to us. Yes, we would get the occasional spanking, but that was a majority of Latino households.

We were escorted into the police station breakroom to eat our Happy Meals. There was silence at the table as we ate our fries and cheeseburgers. Once we finished, they took us into a small interrogation room. It was no more than one hundred square feet with a white, circular table in the center.

One by one, we were asked to follow the officer into a different room for questioning. Rene was the first one taken into the room, then Gabriel, and I was last. All the questions they asked us revolved around whether or not someone burned us. As I waited my turn to go into the room with the investigator, I saw my dad sitting at a distance on a chair in handcuffs.

Growing up in East Hollywood, I had seen adults and teens being detained or arrested. It was kind of normal. But never my parents. My mom's worst fear was for us to fall into gang affiliations, drugs, and vandalism. We were, for the most part, pretty well-behaved and stayed out of trouble outside of our Headquarters.

Hours had gone by, and it must have been well past 9:00 p.m. Between the school nurse, police, investigators, and child services, they had determined these welts on our bodies were cigarette burns. They notified my mom of the events, and we were not going back to Headquarters until further investigation.

The longest I had ever been away from Headquarters at age nine was a night and day during the weekend to spend time at my cousins'. They lived in Korea Town, and that was one of our favorite places to go to because they were about our age. Between video games, trading cards, skating, soccer, and movies, we had plenty to talk about and explore. After this incident, that memory of foster care would fill the space as the longest time the three of us unwillingly stayed away from Headquarters.

We finally left the police station to some other destination. As we drove to wherever they were taking us, we went on the freeway for the first time. There were so many lights, billboards, buildings, and cars traveling in different directions. This all felt new, and I was unable to cry from being so frustrated with our current situation.

All I could think about was running away. The thought petrified me that we would never see my mom again.

We pulled into a single-family residence, and a woman answered the door in a white nightgown and cap. This was supposed to be our temporary Headquarters until there was a ruling for what was going to happen to us. We entered, and they took us into different rooms. Rene and Gabriel shared one, and I was in another.

Were we going to be adopted? What if we never saw our parents? What about school? Were we actually burned? I questioned every bit of reality I thought I knew.

I could not sleep. I stared at the ceiling, wondering what was going to happen and what my mom was doing. This was not a bad dream. I pinched myself, bit myself, and held my breath just to make sure.

We were in a strange place where the ceiling did not have the chipped paint and crack near the west-facing wall I would study every night before falling asleep on our old red carpet. The strangest part about that place was sleeping on a bed. Sleeping on the floor was the norm. The bedroom I was in made me feel claustrophobic.

Nothing made sense. I felt abandoned. How could I not after being removed from our Headquarters and parents without explanation?

Never did anyone explain the events of that incident to us. *It just happened, just because.*

We were officially under foster care from the possibility of neglect and child endangerment. The mosquito bites the nurse and police claimed to be cigarette burns brought us here. This would have been reasonable, except no one burned any of us.

As much as we tried not to scratch, we could not help it. According to our foster care documentation, we remained under foster care for two weeks. The length of time was one giant blur, but I do remember contemplating running away every single day.

Where I was going to run away to was irrelevant so long as I got away from there. I just wanted to get away and back to Headquarters. Sleeping under a freeway seemed better than being in a place I did not understand.

There were several things wrong with this idea. My two living reasons for staying were my siblings. If I ran away, it had to be together, and if we stayed, we were going to make sure we remained together. I was not going to leave them behind.

The day after the police dropped us off, the owner of the house let us know there were Rottweilers serving as guard dogs trained to attack anybody they did not know. They warned us if we tried to run away, these dogs would chase us down. How true was this? No idea.

Knowing there were foster child-eating dogs on the premises did not stop me from contemplating and planning an escape. The first few nights, I remember trying to log the sleeping behaviors of everyone to time when the optimal time to run away would be.

The optimal time was 8:30 p.m. before the alarm was set and right after dinner, when everybody was preoccupied with washing dishes and their night routines. This was our own little version of *Home Alone.*

As small as our studio Headquarters was, that was where I wanted to be. The family who was caring for us did the best they could to try and make us feel welcomed. We were fed, given clothes, allowed to play for hours, and had our own beds.

But I missed the only space I knew, no matter how small it was.

During our time in foster care, we were not allowed to contact the outside world. That meant no computers, no phones, and no letters. I remember rehearsing my home address and home phone number so I wouldn't forget.

In our time there, we were also missing out on our academics. Zoom was not a thing, and to do classwork, we physically had to be there. This gave me a lot of anxiety because I was the salutatorian in the making for my graduating class. I had perfect attendance up until these events.

Rene and I were not allowed to leave, but they would take Gabriel to the grocery store and any other errands the homeowner would do. I tried to convince our caretaker to take us, but someone had clearly tried to run away before. Can you really blame anyone for running away?

Days passed, and we had not heard any news about what would happen to us, when we'd be able to see my mom, and what happened to my dad. This felt a lot like being lost in a Target after wandering off to find the gaming section, except nobody was looking for us, and the Target kept getting bigger and bigger. "I don't know" was the response we regularly received.

My dad was eventually released. When I asked him about the incident as an adult, he had a hard time speaking. My mom would tell me she was extremely devastated, thinking she would not get us back. She made several trips to the police station to investigate what she needed to do.

She consulted one of her friends, Juani. Juani was the mother of my early childhood best friend, Victor, whom I had known since prekindergarten. Juani knew a lot about navigating the world despite being undocumented for a short period of time. It was from Juani the idea of going to the doctor's office to see if there were any medical records about the welts on our bodies that were allegedly cigarette burns.

Sure enough, there was documentation.

Gracias, Medi-Cal.

Mosquitoes infested our apartment during the summer, and we went to the doctor's office to get prescription medicine to help with the itch. Had there been no medical record, we would have remained in the foster care system.

As brief as our foster care experience was, it was enough to foster feelings of abandonment, resentment, and confusion. What would have greatly helped me as a child and teenager would have been talking about the incident. I asked my mom, as an adult, what exactly happened, why we were away for so long, and where Dad went after he was released. I never got a clear answer, and she would change the subject as quickly as she could.

This is perhaps the most frustrating thing about the incident—not having all the answers.

I understand my mom went through something just as traumatic, fearing the loss of her three children while not knowing where to ask for help had it not been for Juani.

The most important part of this experience was my siblings and I stayed together. I do not doubt they could have separated us after being taken to the station, but we weren't. Our situation was a result of untrue accusations, but several decision-makers believed them.

Our Headquarters was not the same after this. My dad no longer lived with us, my mom became stricter about us spending time outside of the home, and I grew up frustrated and angry from not having answers.

CHAPTER 4

SALUTATORIAN

Education was my way out
I ranked second smartest kid in elementary

Traumas forced me deeper into academics
Although I was identified as gifted, it was too late

No fault to my mom
She did what she could with limited knowledge

At least I was the second smartest kid for a bit
It felt good to be seen

According to Urban Dictionary, a salutatorian is "the person who just missed being valedictorian by a few GPA points. A very miserable person indeed. Second place is just the first loser" (Urban Dictionary, 2008).

I first found out I was the second smartest kid in our graduating elementary class about six months after our elections for student government. Our teacher, Ms. McKiver, was a proud African American Christian. I loved her for her charisma and ability to make the classroom come to life with music. Although she did not bestow her personal beliefs onto us, I did adopt many of them for my own—most notably, patriotism.

September 11, 2001, tested our patriotism.

That was the year the attacks on the World Trade Center (WTC) took place. I remember the visual of a tall skyscraper with smoke coming out of it from aerial helicopter coverage. I was up by 5:30 a.m. that day, like I usually was, waiting to shower. The first strike on the towers had just happened. My dad was no longer living with us. All focus remained on the bathroom because there was always a brief window of opportunity for us to use it.

All this was happening while my mom was preparing *huevos rancheros con frijoles y tortillas.*

At 6:00 a.m., the president of the United States, George W. Bush, had given a national address about the events that had just taken place and declared a state of emergency. What happened? Terrorists hijacked a commercial plane and flew it between floors ninety-three and ninety-nine of the North Tower of the WTC in New York City. About an hour later, a second plane was flown right between floors seventy-five and eighty-five of the WTC's South Tower, which was soon followed by an attack on the Pentagon.

By 7:30 a.m., the WTC's North Tower completely collapsed.

Going to school was very strange that day. There was confusion, fear, and anxiety in all of us. Mrs. McKiver began class by addressing the events and having us all take a moment of silence for those who may have lost someone that day. I was raised Catholic, kind of, and was not used to praying in a public setting outside of the church, but I very much enjoyed the comfort we shared with each other. From that moment, our country, communities, and playgrounds would not be the same.

The graduating class theme evolved into patriotism after this event. How could it not? There were visuals of people who were unwilling to burn to death in the towers, deciding to leap out of windows and plunge to their death instead. There were visuals of law enforcement and civilians going into the towers to try to save those who they could reach. Days later, rescuers continued their efforts to try and rescue those in the rubble and identify casualties.

It all seemed like something that should have been a part of an action film, except it wasn't. We were all afraid of what might happen next.

The R. Kelly track "The World's Greatest" was our graduation song. That year, I believed I could be one of the world's greatest. I had no idea how or at what exactly, but I believed I could be.

The idea of creating a student government for our classroom stemmed largely from reinforcing the concepts of democracy, taking the initiative for a greater good, and being proud of the opportunities to serve our country. This sense of patriotism was foreign. Up until then, I didn't always feel like I belonged in *los Estados Unidos*.

On television, I'd see a lot of hate toward people of color and immigrants. My parents were immigrants. Being born in *los Estados Unidos* made us citizens. The government recognized my siblings and I as citizens, but my parents were not. I was always associated with the immigrant populations, whom they would refer to as *mojados, ilegales, y frijoleros.* My feelings were associated with how the world viewed us because of our status.

My parents' illegitimacy in *los Estados Unidos* made me feel like I, too, did not have a place here. On the playground, we would use these slurs to talk to one another, not really understanding the pain many first-generations and immigrants felt as a result. As a child, I remember being the recipient of hate over the color of my skin, and I always found it curious it came from everywhere.

Pre-9/11, while my mom and I were walking down Santa Monica Boulevard on our way to Jons Fresh Marketplace for groceries, I was more energetic than usual. I was excited to be outside and see something other than the four walls we lived in. While skipping, I accidentally bumped into an African American man who lashed out aggressively after making contact. It was an accident, but he did not care.

"Watch where you're going, you wetback. Hey, lady, please watch your baby beaner before I hurt him," he said, approaching us with a menacing grin in his eyes that stretched from ear to ear like the Cheshire Cat.

One of our neighbors was walking right behind us and caught a glimpse of what was happening. He was from Chile, but most people thought he was African American because of the color of his skin. He stood up for us and asked the man to stop. The man backed away, and we were kept from harm.

In another instance, I was in a Target browsing through the trading card section, contemplating what Pokémon booster packs to buy, and then the music section to listen to music at one of the booths. A white male clerk was following me around and made it obvious he was watching me. He eventually approached me to say, "Just to make sure another beaner isn't going to steal from us, I will take these cards to the register. Meet me there when you are ready to pay and try not to steal anything on your way to the register."

I left the store empty-handed.

In a final example, we were playing Heads Up, Seven Up in our classroom. The objective of the game is to guess who tapped your thumb while everyone had their heads down on the table. I was one of the chosen ones for this game, and before the game started, one of the girls, a fair-skinned Latina, commented she did not want any dark Mexicans to select her. She stared right at me.

These events happened when I was a kid, and I always had the impression I did not belong because I was dark, Mexican, and the child of immigrant parents. I never understood or really saw the benefit of being a citizen until the fifth grade.

Being recognized as salutatorian meant I was seen for something other than the color of my skin, my ethnicity, and being the child of immigrant parents. I did what I was supposed to, and school came naturally to me. Never did my parents say, "Mijo, you will be salutatorian."

Sometime between the events of September 11 and New Year's, Mrs. McKiver arranged for a parent-teacher conference with my mom. The reason was unclear, but she was very adamant about this happening, and it seemed like something that had been on her mind for a while.

My mother agreed to meet with her.

"Ms. Clara Luna, your son is gifted and should not be here. He would be much better with students who undergo academic rigor to develop their talents further," Mrs. McKiver urged.

"What do you mean, teacher? Is my son struggling in class?" my mom questioned the recommendation, thinking Mrs. McKiver was alluding I may be a special needs student.

"Oh no, my apologies. Quite the contrary, your son belongs to a gifted program. I don't understand how he made it this far without being tested for being gifted. He has aptitudes that seem effortless when compared to other students. I think he has a real shot at being something great, and it's worth looking into."

I was gifted?

After giving us this news, Mrs. McKiver made calls to figure out what she could do. She found out I was too old to qualify for any gifted programs as gifted students had to be identified during second and third grade to allow for the nurturing of their gifts.

The National Association for Gifted Children suggests by testing a child early, they can also retest at a later time, which is especially important for those institutions that may be ESL and of low socioeconomic status. Our demographic often gets overlooked. Federally funded research shows gifted children living in poverty and from ethnic and language minority groups are 250 percent less likely to be identified for and serve in gifted programs in their schools, even when they achieve at the same level as their more affluent identified peers (Islas, 2017). I was a part of the 250 percent who went unidentified.

I was an unidentified gifted student.

Being a part of the gifted program would have been interesting and could have meant skipping a grade or two. Despite this discovery not going anywhere, it was nice to feel like I was seen. Not having been enrolled in specialized programs was a true test of my gifts. Whether or not I would acknowledge and nurture my gifts on my own as I developed into an adult was going to be my responsibility and testament to those gifts.

Having been salutatorian of my graduating class was a statement for, "I will be all right, I got this, and I am up to something."

There were instances where my gifts may have presented themselves, and though they were not obvious then, they manifested in different ways.

In kindergarten, playtime was one of the most critical ways to socialize us children, to become collaborative and cooperative members of society. During playtime, I was the alleged playtime organizer. The kids would look to me to organize them during playtime into different groups. The organizing was not the most impressive part, though. The fact they listened was. What can I say? I was born to lead. The comment of this event was given to my mom by my kindergarten teacher, Ms. Lee.

Introducing order and schedules was important in first and second grade. I remember Mrs. Jaramillo, my first and second-grade teacher, would have our daily schedule on the chalkboard. I loved to go to school and learn, but I loved playtime even more. Since work was partitioned into increments of thirty to sixty minutes, I figured out I could finish a majority of the classwork by lunchtime and spend the remainder of the day playing.

I remember zooming through the work to move on to the next task. What made no sense to me was why a task that could be accomplished in ten minutes was stretched out for an hour. Finishing my work as quickly as possible to reap the reward of playtime was what I lived for those two years. There was nothing stopping me from accomplishing this.

Then there was the third-grade experience where I was an entrepreneur selling Pokémon cards with the goal of making money so my mom could spend more time with us. My mom and dad never talked to us about entrepreneurship or business, but somehow, that came naturally. Between my great-grandparents, grandparents, and mother, there was a history of entrepreneurship. For my parents, it was coffee, and for me, it was *esos mugrosos* Pokémon cards.

In the ideal scenario, a child would have been recognized as gifted to receive an appropriate education and further develop those manifested gifts. In my eyes, the greatest gift of all was being able to experience the world as the rest of my peers. I am not bitter or upset about not being properly identified as gifted. On the contrary, I believe who I am today is better off from not having been in those programs. Graduating second in my class during elementary was the first of the future successes I could eventually manifest on my own.

Before we arrived at our graduation, we had to undergo our version of democracy. Running for office was on a nomination basis, and I was one of the chosen ones.

I was nominated for vice president. Preparing for a speech was difficult because I had no idea what I wanted to do if elected or what I wanted to talk about. More recess? Movie day to be every other week for the entire classroom, not just those who were performing well? Everyone to be awarded a pass to have a failed test or homework be forgiven? I thought this last idea was actually pretty brilliant, but I was thinking way too logically about elections.

The closing remarks of one of the other nominated vice presidents left a strong impression. "If elected vice president, I will wash Mrs. McKiver's car."

Just like that, Orlando took the vice presidency. Orlando was known to be a funny guy, and this was probably the most epic win in student government history. I was relieved I was not going to be held accountable for those responsibilities.

This was great preparation for the subsequent speeches to follow because being salutatorian meant I also had to prepare a speech for our graduating ceremony.

I had a difficult time putting a story together to conclude our elementary school and commence the next chapter. Expressing gratitude went without saying. What I realized was I placed a large amount of importance on my elementary school friends. Belonging was extremely important. This is perhaps the most natural human need. In my salutatorian speech, the importance of friends showed when I acknowledged a majority of my class by name.

Giving this speech was a great lesson about knowing, in the end, I needed to become independent and mind my own business, meaning I am the priority. Part of the want to address everyone by name came from the request from everyone asking, "Who is your best friend?" I did not have a best friend.

When I transitioned to middle school, I didn't have any friends. Those same friends I mentioned by name ghosted me in middle school.

CHAPTER 5

LEAVING HEADQUARTERS

———

There was no second-guessing leaving Headquarters
To grow and thrive, the option was obvious

My parents must have experienced the same leaving
Mexico
They must have been nervous

I was extremely nervous
All I would live on was Maruchan

Thirty-year-old me thanks seventeen-year-old me
Leaving was messy, and it was great

———

After my dad was forbidden to come home due to the foster care incident, middle school was confusing and full of teenage angst. To catch you up without wallowing for too long, the friends I had in elementary school ghosted me. I started off middle school as a loner. I was four-foot-ten and about one hundred fifty-five pounds. I was not the least bit athletic, and I battled a severe case of acne that had me looking like a Freddy Krueger stunt double. My acne was so bad I remember googling, "At what age will I be good looking?" Google returned a website designed to tell you when your time would come. According to the website, my time would come at age seventeen. I patiently waited for seventeen.

I have very vague memories of middle school. Three years feels eternal when you have no sense of identity.

Like in engineering, the best way to figure who I may have been was through iterations. Iterating meant taking on different identities to determine the best fit. Middle school was a lot like speed dating with myself, except it was a bit more permanent and involved lots of roleplaying. All these identities remain with me in some way, and some of the biggest identities began with questions like, "Was I or could I be a rocker, a gangbanger, a nerd, or a beaner? What about all of them at the same time?"

I took pride in my music of choice between screamo, hardcore, and metalcore because of their heavy guitar riffs, hardcore drum breakdowns, and pig squealing for vocals. I dressed the part in my liberty spikes, skinny jeans, Chucks, and chains. I felt connected because I felt different. I continued to feel out of place with the mainstream. There was pride in being different without limits. Yes, the music could be loud and angry, but that was therapeutic. My taste in music was partly how I was introduced to gangs.

I wanted to be a gangbanger, but my cousins kept me away because they genuinely believed I had a bright future. I was attracted to this future because it seemed to bring protection, respect, and brotherhood, which I needed to find my identity. The few gangbangers I knew made it feel cool. They would give each other props for messing around the neighborhood or entertaining themselves. In contrast, my dad never acknowledged anything I did.

In middle school, I had no interest in hooking up and meeting girls, getting wasted at parties, or going to backyard shows. Instead, my interest was protection from bullying. In a span of two weeks, I had four brand-new black JanSport backpacks stolen while I was playing basketball. I never found out who did it, but I knew if I had backup, my backpacks would not have been touched. I remember trying to prevent it by buying a combination lock and tying it around the basketball pole. This did not work, so I stopped playing outright.

There were times I avoided going to school early because there was one kid who would wait outside my first period to rough me up. I arrived at school early twice, and in one instance, there were two kids hanging out beside my classroom. One of them placed me in a headlock I managed to get out of, his friend a lookout while this was happening. Although they did not beat me up, I knew if I showed up, I would be a target.

I imagined by rolling up with a group that had your back, you were basically untouchable, which was true to an extent. Rivalries between gangs would make any protection seem obsolete because everyone was a target. We just knew who had more street cred and an ability to get away with certain things.

There were no male role models in my life, so this was how I filled that gap. To this day, I am forever grateful to my cousins for keeping me away and not allowing me to be jumped into gang life. The offer was presented, but I declined each time, as my cousins would look at me and shake their heads.

To avoid further bullying, I was an incognito nerd. Failing classes and not caring about school was cool. Being book smart was considered weak and made you an easy target. My fight-or-flight instinct told me to avoid any situation that might attract bullying, which meant pleading ignorance to my intelligence. Did I ever brag or bring up I was salutatorian at my elementary school? Not once! By no means was I Harvard material, but I believed I could get into a community college. While I was trying to figure out my identity, I was also on a mission to survive my youth.

Then there was the subject of race that evolved from who was the fastest on the playground into who your family was and what neighborhood you grew up in. It was Latinos versus Latinos, Latinos versus blacks, Latinos versus whites, Latinos versus Armenians, and the list went on. It was all unnecessary, but the hostility against one another was there. This period of my development also marked an embarrassment with my place of origin and low socioeconomic status. I was embarrassed I was low socioeconomic, first-generation, Mexican American, and my parents were dishwashers and housekeepers.

I hated being poor. I hated not having answers. I hated being Mexican. I hated feeling like there was no life outside the three-hundred-fifty-square-foot Headquarters we lived in.

Admitting I was embarrassed to be seen in public with my mom is painful. I loved my mom, but the trigger for embarrassment was my mom recycled and carried a plastic bag with her so she could pick plastic bottles and aluminum cans. Money was money, and I knew every little bit mattered for us. There were times we would be seen doing this, and the slurs would bombard us. *Beaner. Go back to your country. Wetbacks.*

None of this was explained to me growing up. *Nomas paso y ya paso.*

Looking into the past, although not an excuse, I realized the pain of struggling with my identity made me into the professional, role model, and confident person I am today. My household was two-parent until it wasn't. The period of single parenthood my mother endured fueled my struggle with identity and teenage angst. I know I could have been a better eldest sibling if I had better understood my feelings and experiences.

Mental health was not a priority in my or many first-generation Latino households I knew.

We never revisited the incidents when we were in foster care with my parents. Whenever we mentioned it, my mom pretended it never happened.

Mental health was simply not in our vocabulary. I remember my dad's solution to most things that were troubling was *no te gastes el cerebro pensando tanto*, which means *don't waste your brain thinking so much*. Dismissing those feelings was not the solution. I needed the professional help, but first, I had to survive.

Let's fast-forward through the five most troubling years between middle school and early high school.

Junior and senior year in high school were my favorites because I was becoming proud of my identity. I cared less and less about what others' impressions of me were. I was five foot six, one hundred fifty-five pounds, athletic, and no longer suffered from acne. I loved being with the soccer guys because I loved the sport. I'd eventually build the courage to try out for volleyball my junior year despite the disapproval from some of my friends. I had no experience, and I really wanted to try out a new sport. When the soccer guys found out, without hesitation, they decided the sport was "gay."

The resistance was because it was considered a "girl's sport." Volleyball is actually a very physically demanding sport that requires a lot of strength, agility, and critical thinking. I developed an aptitude in a short time practicing the sport. I felt I was cheated out of varsity my first year because my coach was playing favorites, but it's okay because junior varsity was fun too. This was a great journey into more hidden talents I was unaware of.

What can I say about my late teens? I was definitely confident about my decisions and willing to explore. While I was in high school, I'd often be gone late into the night, hanging out with friends, visiting girlfriends at other schools, and seeing something different. Having a student bus pass opened up a large part of Los Angeles I would have otherwise not known about.

I never fell into drugs, addiction, or criminal activity, and that gave my mom the extra peace of mind I would be all right when leaving Headquarters for university. Of course, leaving did not come without resistance.

"No te tienes que mover," my mom would adamantly suggest.

"Me tengo que mover para poder avanzar. Es la única manera," I countered, trying to have my mom see my ambition to leave was under the premise of becoming better.

"Quien te va a cuidar?"

"Lo averiguaré yo mismo. Nos enseñaste que hay solución para todo."

"Y si te pasa algo?"

"Voy a averiguarlo. Si me quedo aquí me pasará algo. Si me voy, me pasará algo. Suceden cosas y lo averiguaremos."

We had this conversation more than seven times in the months leading up to my departure to university. There was no denying I had it good at Headquarters. My mom practically raised us on her own, making sure we had food, shelter, doctor visits, and *caldo de pollo* to make us feel better when we were sick. My mom made a strong case for me not to leave because adulting was expensive, but that was not reason enough for me to stop myself short by staying.

While I was applying to universities, I considered living in a dorm to become assimilated to campus culture and college life. Being homesick was not a consideration, but I noticed I was subconsciously applying to schools that were close enough to home in case I wanted to visit on weekends.

Earning my driver's license was a foreshadowing of being able to leave for university. I took advantage of the fact our high school offered drivers education early in the mornings. Waking up early was nothing new, so why not earn a driver's license in the process? This would open up my university options once I began applying.

UC Riverside, UC San Bernardino, and California State University, Northridge (CSUN) were the only schools I seriously applied to because those were the schools I believed I could get into with little effort. My school of choice was CSUN, considering the cost of tuition, cost of living, and proximity to Headquarters.

I applied to UC Santa Barbara, UCLA, UC San Diego, and Harvard as longshots, not giving my admission package a lot of thought. Money for the applications was not an issue because being from a low-income household meant we had waivers. Had I taken my applications more seriously, my acceptance into more prestigious institutions may have been possible.

Finances played a big role in my decision-making. Our high school college counselor, Mrs. Campbell, advised us Cal States were generally cheaper than UCs, and UCs were generally cheaper than private institutions. Although we had FAFSA, there was growing concern if there was any need for additional money. I would have to take student loans because there was no way my parents could support me financially. I should have paid more attention to grants and scholarships.

Growing up, I believed debt was evil. My parents did not have any debt and paid for everything in cash. In our culture, the Latinx community, there was a lot of pride in being able to pay in cash. There was no way I would be able to pay for school with all cash. So, taking student loans was going to be necessary, which meant I would want to take the least amount possible in student loans.

"Mijo, piensa cuánto dinero vas a ahorrar viviendo con nosotros," my mom said, placing a large emphasis on the money involved to my adulting equation.

"I know I would save a lot, but I really do not want to spend my time in traffic. I also want to experience more than just living here," I said with a continued belief and emphasis that time spent on things other than driving was going to be valuable. The truth was I just wanted to be away from Headquarters.

"Al final del día será tu decisión y te apoyaremos. Y sabes muy bien que aquí tienes un hogar. Lo único que queremos es que no te estreses demasiado."

"Thanks, Mom. I am sure this is what I need to do. Once I move, I do not plan on moving back, not because I do not want to, but out of respect and to continue the path of independence."

"Está bien."

Naturally, I thought about everything that could go wrong. What if I did not have enough money to pay for my food, gas, rent, insurance, books, etc.? I knew these would be some of the many expenses I would face once I was on my own. What if I got into an accident? How would I pay for my medical or death expenses? Yes, my mind really went there. There was no denying being away from home was going to be expensive, and I was okay with that.

As much as I wanted to work, my mom made a conscious effort to prevent it because she was afraid the money would be a distraction from my academics. When I asked her if this had anything to do with her experience of putting her education on hold, coming to the United States, and never leaving after working and having children, I realized it had everything to do with this. She did not want this to be my reality.

Without ever saying it, she was trying to protect us.

This yearning to work began from childhood and followed me to these moments as I prepared myself to leave Headquarters. I was trained to be frugal, think twice about unnecessary expenses, and save as much as possible in case something terrible happened.

The moment I realized I was actually leaving Headquarters was when I drove to the dorm's office in Northridge, CA, to drop off my deposit. Ironically, this was also the first time I took the freeway after passing my driver's license exam and being gifted a car as a going away and graduation gift. I was pulled over and ticketed for tailgating. Later that same day, I was also ticketed for failing to read the street signs and parking in a space that had street cleaning that same day.

To make matters worse, I left my headlights on and came back to a parking ticket and a dead battery.

Welcome to adulthood, Bartholomew!

Okay, it wasn't the greatest introduction to independence, but I had to start learning somehow. To this day, reading those street signs is like trying to go through the terms and conditions after downloading a new app on a smartphone.

I didn't have much to take with me. Actually, I probably had more food than personal belongings. My parents helped me pack and move. Driving from Little Armenia to Northridge took about thirty minutes. The great part about move-in day was there were several student organizations out to help with the move.

Spending my first night on a bed of my own, no matter how uncomfortable, was a luxury I was unaccustomed to. I briefly relived the same feelings I had from being on a bed of my own in my time at foster care, except this time, it was of my own accord. Leaving was the single best decision I could have made for my future. Otherwise, I would have never left.

My biggest hope was for my siblings to follow in my footsteps and eventually muster the courage to leave. They never did, and to this day, they have not, which makes me believe I would not have either.

STAGE TWO

WE ARE
SUPPOSED TO

DECIDING ON A MAJOR

My majors of interest were business and engineering
Intuitively, I felt I did not have to major in business to
practice business

Unconsciously, I felt I could one day leverage engineering
skills
If a photon can shake a universe, why can't leveraged skills

My focus was being able to define possible
I didn't know it, but I was up to something

Engineering would go on to become excellent leverage
Business would go on to become emergent

Every year, we visit our academic advisers to outline our
coursework to get us closer to commencement and into real-
life. During my undergrad, it was essential to find a balance
between academics, work, social life, community involvement, rest, and relaxation. After all, college was a time for
growth, exploration, and fun. I gave myself permission to
join different interest groups like Sigma Lambda Beta, New
Student Orientation, Salsa Libre Dance Team, Hermanos

Unidos, and the Society of Hispanic Professional Engineers (SHPE).

In my first two years at CSUN, I was strategically undeclared, so I would have the opportunity to explore majors before committing to one. I have to thank Mrs. Campbell and Ms. Brown at Hollywood High School for this piece of advice because they made it known *it's okay not to know what path we want to take going into university.*

I heard stories of people changing majors. It was great knowing there was flexibility, but I did not want to invest my time taking credits I would not need. Most of all, I did not want to find myself dissatisfied with a career I was allegedly preparing myself for. Deciding on a major appeared to be an end-all-be-all decision that would determine my fate after graduation.

It felt that way, at least, especially with student loans being a factor.

Being first-generation meant I was at the disadvantage of not having immediate family members to reach out to for perspective or advice. Organizations like Sigma Lambda Beta provided a brotherhood of Latino-based multicultural brothers who were also first-generation from different majors with similar backgrounds who were also trying to figure it all out. Organizations like SHPE shared resources, mentorship, leadership development, and a vision of the future many of us first-generation students could one day benefit from and embody.

To augment the magnanimity of how real this decision was, I would ask myself, "What do I want to do for the next forty years?" This then provoked the question, "Do I really want to dedicate myself to one thing for forty years?"

That seemed so permanent. Almost illogical, but it was the only reality I knew about.

A major was supposed to help kickstart the unraveling of my career.

I shared my progression with my parents when I visited, so they felt engaged. They did not always understand, but I know they were at least happy knowing I was doing what I wanted. When I left Headquarters, I made a commitment to maintaining a relationship with my parents and siblings.

"Bueno, piensa en qué carrera quieres cuando termines la escuela." My mom would encourage me that any decision I made was the right one.

"The only problem I have is I'm not sure what I want to do after university," I would say with hesitation and concern.

"¿Que es lo que te interesa?"

"Math and science. And business."

"¿Y qué se puede hacer con la ciencia y las matemáticas?"

"Build cars, do research, or maybe become a professor? I think that's it."

"Lo ves. Ay opciones en todo esto."

"Seems like it. Next time I visit my college adviser, I will make sure to ask about math and science majors that might be a good fit for me."

Being first-generation means we don't readily know the options or opportunities available to us. There are plenty of options, but we don't know what we don't know.

Unless we have older siblings, cousins, mentors, role models, or advisers, we really don't have a clue of what is possible. We go with the flow and figure it all out as we go along. This can be a blessing. It means we are more willing to explore and take risks. This may come from the ignorance involved in not understanding our options.

We all had academic catalogs to reference, but that thing was the size of *Webster's Dictionary.* I only had it because it was required material for every incoming freshman. The logical thing to do would have been to open the book and map out my future using the roadmap given. I didn't. Instead, I waited until my adviser meetings to make my decisions.

Besides the conversation with my mom, I did very little to prepare for this meeting because I knew there would be a discussion on the possible options for me.

Bayramian Hall at the CSUN campus was where I would go see my adviser because I was undeclared and part of the Educational Opportunity Program (EOP). They provided us with resources like scholarships, tutoring, and professional development, all critical services I could have taken better advantage of.

My commute to campus was five minutes from a local residence a few of us decided to rent out and split. Every morning, I made certain to overpack so I would not have to go back to Headquarters—all my books, my gym bag, my lunch, and a change of clothes in the event I had to stay at a friend's place. Today was going to be the day I made the big boy decision of selecting a major. I imagined this feeling was like Ash Ketchum selecting his starter Pokémon with Professor Oak.

My time management was subpar because I was everywhere and nowhere. Between my student involvement, working at the Jewish Studies Department, my other part-time jobs, and finishing my coursework, I did not make much time for myself. I was often stressed out and on the brink of burning out. Being at university meant trying to do as much as possible before I graduated.

The student advisers advised me well with their recommendations of coursework like Chicano studies, music, theater, history, and math. In one of my Chicano studies courses, for example, I learned from the book *The Revolt of the Cockroach People* that a news reporter played a big role in the development of a voice for the Chicano/a community in the late 1980s. I also learned CSUN, formerly known as San Fernando State, was one of the hotspots for the Chicano/a community in developing a voice in Los Angeles County, which was why there was a strong faculty base in Chicano studies at CSUN.

This student advisement was different because the first question I was asked by the adviser was, "Have you thought about which major you want to declare?"

I knew I was leaning toward math and science only because of how natural it came to me. The subject matter was fairly easy, so the majors must be too, right?

My GPA was above a 3.5. After my salutatorian experience in elementary school, I considered myself a B+ student. A four was great and all, but that was way more effort than I would have liked to give.

Engineering. This was the word that would redirect my studies and careers of choice. More importantly, the word "engineering" helped me adopt a mindset for agility, systems, and continued learning.

The word "engineering" came up in my conversation with my adviser. Frankly, I had a vague idea of what engineering really was or could be. It was, in my mind, train conducting or programming—nothing more, nothing less.

Should it have been obvious there were dozens of disciplines of engineering? If it was, it wasn't obvious to me.

"Engineering can be many things. At CSUN, we offer mechanical, civil, electrical, computer, and manufacturing engineering. To be honest, I don't know much about the major either, but if you think about technology, it's the engineers who make all of it happen," said the adviser trying to put engineering into perspective. I never realized how many disciplines there actually were, and this was only our campus. There was petroleum, agriculture, materials, logistics, testing, software, aeronautics, radar, propulsion, electrical, hardware, and the list went on to various sub-disciplines within those disciplines.

Two days was all the time I had to decide. So, I did the most logical thing—consult Google.

I searched for, "What do engineers do?"

From this search, websites like Indeed convinced me engineering might be for me. Search results read something like:

- Engineers use math and science to solve problems and make use of new discoveries.
- Engineers make use of information to find practical uses.
- Engineers pursue valuable innovations that advance the way humans use products.
- Engineers can work with everything from massive architectural constructions to complex maps of the human genome.

This took me to deeper into: "What are some of the best engineering companies to work for?"

- Google
- Microsoft
- Boeing
- Ford
- BMW
- Northrop Grumman

And the next search: "What sort of technologies and products do engineering companies make?"

- Aircraft
- Medical Devices
- Satellites
- Engines
- Spacecraft

According to *Forbes* magazine, the top three highest-earning bachelor's degrees in 2015 on average were electrical engineering, computer engineering, and mechanical engineering at a starting salary of fifty-six thousand dollars per year (Adams, 2014).

I was sold after reading I could potentially work on cutting-edge technologies and make a difference in the world. I mean, who doesn't fantasize about being Tony Stark, building the future *while* being able to contribute to the community? Just me?

The Society of Hispanic Professional Engineers (SHPE) taught me I was not the only one. The membership was largely first-generation Hispanics who were on a mission to better themselves and the community.

Before that moment, I did not completely realize engineers are necessary in almost every facet of society. Everything inside and outside our homes, advancements in wellbeing, sanitation, travel, music, communication, vacations, fitness—literally everything has been touched by an engineer at some level.

When I began considering salary, it completely blew my mind! Engineers made four to five times what the minimum wage was. My amazement came from knowing my Head-quarters, growing up, only knew the minimum wage of five dollars and fifty cents. This was an extremely big deal, but it wasn't everything.

On average, STEM-based careers make more than any other profession out of university. STEM workers who majored in a STEM field in college typically made higher salaries than those who did not. On average, 101,100 dollars vs. 87,600 dollars (Day, 2021). I saw this as the perfect opportunity to advance from the low socioeconomic status I was born into. It's not that all my decisions were based on money, but these decisions now had a nice, steady income associated with them.

I'd declare mechanical engineering because when I asked my friends about flexibility, mechanical seemed to have a broader curriculum than others. In university, you learned a bit about everything as a mechanical engineer. There were courses in electrical engineering, programming, comput-er-aided design (CAD), finite element analysis (FEA), robot-ics, machine design, and thermodynamics.

Emerging technology had my interest, but I knew very little about it. Granted, I did not know what to look for, but I knew things were happening in the world somewhere.

Google Images really fed my imagination. I saw planes, spacecraft, robotics, medical devices, computers, drones, ships, satellites, and self-driving vehicles. Deciding on mechanical engineering was the best academic decision I could have made.

CHAPTER 7

AND WE ARE...
TAKE XXIII

———

Twelve strangers came together to develop a story
The premise were the themes of transitions, relationships,
body abuse, and prejudice

The beauty in our performance was it was real and true
We relived our stories for two weeks

This was the first time most of us openly shared traumas
Our closing message was: "It gets better"

It did

———

My first day on the CSUN campus in August 2009 for student
orientation was welcoming and exciting. I remember the level
of energy of everyone in a red polo was that of Road Runner's
speed and authenticity of Bugs Bunny.

Orientation Leaders (OLs), the red polo road-running bun-
nies, were at the forefront of acclimating incoming students

to the CSUN campus. From the way I felt welcomed, I wanted to welcome others.

We were known as the red army because whenever we all congregated, we literally were in uniform. The standard was a sleek red polo, black pants or shorts, and nearly unlimited energy like the Energizer Bunny.

Anyone and everyone became an orientation leader for one or two reasons:

1. A need to give back from immense pride and appreciation for the CSUN campus and experience.
2. To benefit from priority registration the following semester.

Both were legitimate reasons, but reason number one kept us all together.

Reason number two became more common after the realization there were more students than seats in a classroom. This forced students to compete for classes, making priority registration a high motivator to secure full-time status. For many of us, not having full-time status meant potentially losing federal student aid toward tuition.

I was enrolled in the GE Honors program, so I bypassed this experience, but I had many friends who were not so fortunate. The first few days of class were flooded with students waiting to receive a registration form or be placed on a waiting list. Although this perk of priority registration was given, OL's remained committed after receiving the benefit because they genuinely wanted to help.

Being an OL came with the responsibility of mentoring, attending leadership trainings, and supporting commencement, orientation, president's picnic, and freshman convocation. Each event was a milestone in the journey a student would experience in their time at CSUN.

Within the orientation community, there were different tiers of contributors: orientation leaders, matador mentors, student coordinators, and TAKE cast members. Orientation Leader was the entry-level role, mentors the experienced role, and student coordinators were the equivalent of management. This last group, the TAKE cast, was a distinguished group responsible for performing on the subjects of relationships, body abuse, transitions, and prejudice incoming students, or someone they know, may have faced or will face in some way, shape, or form.

Being a TAKE cast member was more than just a performance. The TAKE performance promoted university resources and services through real-life situations and scenarios as experienced by the cast. The stories we performed were ours.

The audience watching this performance consisted of incoming freshmen, transfer students, faculty, and staff over the course of two weeks. Yes, the TAKE cast would go on to become local celebrities. To leap from orientation leader to TAKE cast member was not something I planned to do, but I gave it consideration after a friend suggested I apply. There was an extensive interview process that required vulnerability in answering what we had learned from our experiences, an ability to express our adversities and outcomes, the advice we would give to the incoming student population, and how these experiences could further develop us as leaders. Part of the objective was to have a diverse group of students who could capture the essence of the CSUN campus.

The story I shared was about being a low socioeconomic status, first-generation Latino born to immigrant parents, and being a foster care youth. I'd talk about how leaving Headquarters for CSUN was my step forward from the world I grew up in, and I was trying to set an example for my siblings. I had a hard time believing my story could be relevant. Talking about my story felt like a rerun of *Sábado Gigante* or *El Chavo del Ocho*. I could not accept there was another individual who would want to listen to something that happens everywhere.

I wrote my essays for my application and finally accepted the story I put down on paper was the best I could do.

How many of us grow up not having role models or examples of what is possible? My first-generation, person of color, Mexican American, low socioeconomic, STEM student, and male identities were calling me to service.

Applying meant making myself vulnerable to rejection.

Finding the courage to apply came from the experience of trying something that brought me just as much anxiety: riding a bicycle through campus. I learned how to ride a bike late in life, around my early twenties, and learning how to stop was the most difficult for me. As a result, one day, while I was riding on campus to the library, I ended up circling the building three times, trying to figure out how to come to a resting stop.

The moment finally came. Instead of braking, I approached a recycling bin beside a handicap ramp on the west side of the building that brought me to a resting stop upon impact. I wasn't hurt, and nobody witnessed the event.

The moral of the story is just do it! The worst thing that can happen is circling a building three times and finding a nice recycling bin to brake with.

Onstage, the idea of forgetting the line was petrifying. I forgot lines, and I learned to use the first words that came to mind—thank you, castmates, for not leaving me hanging. I was thinking further ahead than I should have been. Extensive training and rehearsals prepared us for this sort of thing.

Once I overcame my doubt, sharing my story seemed like something someone else could empathize with. If one life would have been impacted in the process, then applying for the opportunity to share my story would have been worth it.

My interviewers—Christopher, assistant director of the program, and Krystal, TAKE cast director—put me at ease. I was not prepared for the emotions that consumed the interview room.

Between the experiences of being a first-generation college student, person of color, foster care youth, and born to immigrant parents who came from a low socioeconomic status, Christopher and Krystal reassured me there was a story to tell. For the first time, I genuinely felt like my story mattered.

Hearing myself speak was how I realized my story was an extension of my parents' story and the dreams and aspirations they once held. I was not an immigrant, but I felt much more connected to the undocumented community I grew up with. Filling out applications asking me about my citizenship made me feel like an impostor.

About a month later, I received my acceptance email into TAKE XXIII. I was dumbfounded and in disbelief. I would later find out there was another applicant who was highly considered before I interviewed, but my interview changed everything.

The lesson here is, despite all odds, go and interview. Shoot your shot because you will miss one hundred percent of the ones we don't take.

There were twelve of us in the cast. This group was Headquarters. We gave each other support, sympathy, ideas, and the strength to come to terms with stories we had not been able to share. Some of us knew one another, and some were complete strangers. The beauty of it all was none of us knew what to expect from the process. We spent a lot of time together to learn more about each other. At the same time, as our stage personas developed, we became better acquainted with ourselves.

A lot of feeling vomit was necessary to tell what we went through collectively. Our audience was supposed to connect to the themes of body abuse, prejudice, relationships, and transitions. Our emphasis on transitions focused on themes of helicopter parents, being caught up with social life, and not being able to make friends. Our story of relationships revolved around infidelity, pregnancy, and STDs. When it came to body abuse, we explored our image of fit and healthy, self-mutilation, and suicide. Finally, the theme of prejudice touched all of us when we considered stereotypes of our different cultures.

If you asked me what I enjoyed most about acting, it would have to be connecting with feelings I have either not felt in a long time or I did not know I was capable of experiencing. It felt great to feel love, anger, frustration, despair, melancholy, bliss, and ignorance, all within a matter of a year.

Acting was a necessary break from engineering. Being on stage let me see having to be right or wrong and not allowing feelings to take center stage was exhausting. I found allowing myself to feel was the best medicine there ever was. All the pent-up frustrations and emotions from the last nineteen years were finally able to roam freely.

I guess feeling was part of being human.

CHAPTER 8

LEARNING FROM LOVE

———

Despite popular belief, engineers have feelings
We are just as capable of breaking hearts and susceptible to
heartbreak

It is great to have been acquainted with vulnerability
From my two most memorable experiences with love

The outcomes were important
Learn to love myself first

Taking an eight-year hiatus from love was essential
Love, and the lack thereof, helped me channel my energy

———

At the first sign of feelings, I sprint away faster than Usain
Bolt. Love is messy, irrational, and means potentially getting
hurt. I would much rather study relentlessly for a difficult
engineering exam than try to make a relationship work.

For most of my young adult life, I left one relationship for
another. I never gave myself time to be alone and focus on my
own interests, ambitions, and goals. When it came to really

committing, part of me felt by having someone, my journey would be less lonely.

In Spanish, there is a saying: *mejor solo a que mal acompañado*. "It is better to be alone than in terrible company." Admitting I had to work on myself first was difficult, but it had to be done. There were plenty of options ready to commit, but I was not.

My last two serious relationships were the most painfully necessary and impactful. I took my relationship with Gina for granted. She was the one who got away because of my irresponsibility and inability to appreciate love. Stacey took me for granted in all the ways I was in my relationship with Gina.

Okay, you are wondering, just as I am, what exactly does romance have to do with STEM and my journey toward becoming a multicareer professional? Everything! Admitting to my unhealthy relationship with romance was the first step toward:

1. Loving myself.
2. Being open and honest with partners.

By practicing romance more honestly, I have been able to set clearer boundaries for achieving my highest potential and creating an environment where love may actually be possible.

Since age twenty-two, I've remained single. This decision has helped me remain focused on all of my important professional, private, and interpersonal experiences.

GINA

When I first met Gina, I was not the slightest bit interested.
I knew she was in my Chicano Studies 100 class, but I only
noticed her interpreter. It was only after the universe forced
us to meet—running into each other in three different
instances on the same day—did I notice *her*. First, the ele-
vator in Bayramian Hall, next the Matador Bookstore, and
finally, the courtyard outside of Bayramian Hall. We both
thought this was a strange coincidence and stopped at the
courtyard to talk.

The next thirty minutes we spent writing to one another out
of my blue spiral notebook would set us up for a relationship.
We did not let a language barrier come between us after we
realized the universal language we had working for us was...
love.

People were far more curious about her than I was. Gina's
outer beauty could attract most who looked her way—it could
bring traffic to a stop faster than any siren passing through an
intersection. I could not see the beauty they did. The quality
that drew me in was laughter. Have you ever heard a laugh
that was the right frequency, pitch, tone, length, and echo?
That was Gina's.

She never stopped laughing and made sure to enjoy every
waking moment. If there was ever a dull moment, she made
sure to adventure the heck out of it.

American Sign Language (ASL) was not yet in my repertoire.
Before Gina came along, I had a curiosity to learn ASL but

never enough motivation to actually learn. I began with a ten-minute alphabet crash course on YouTube I played over and over again to show her the following day I could spell my name. Gina never asked me to learn her language. I wanted to immerse myself more into her world, and language was just one way to do it.

CSUN had a nationally recognized and famous deaf studies program, which was how I got some of my deaf coursework done. Yes, I considered double majoring in engineering and deaf studies.

During the 2012 fall semester, I was taking Introduction to Deaf Studies and Numerical Analysis of Engineering Systems. This combination triggered my entrepreneurial mind.

That was the semester I learned about cochlear implants, which is a sound processor worn behind the ear that uses a transmitter to send sound signals to a receiver and stimulator implanted under the skin, stimulating the auditory nerve with electrodes. This was a very controversial operation and technology, which is how I came up with the idea of an app to help the deaf and hearing community communicate.

At the core of the cochlear technology was a solution to communication.

My early experience of writing on paper, typing messages, and texting with Gina made me feel like there was a need for such an app. I did not do market research, but I just figured others might have found themselves in a similar predicament.

I brought this idea to my Numerical Analysis professor during his office hours. I presented the idea and expected some guidance, but that was out of his realm of subject matter. He told me the idea and intention was great, but I needed some development, prototype, market research to be able to present something and then iterate on the app.

The problem I wanted to solve was a communication barrier between the deaf and hearing communities. Only after having been introduced to this new culture was I able to acknowledge the need. I did not develop the idea further, but I was astounded to find there were several apps developed for the deaf community. Those apps included Ava, RogerVoice, Sound Amplifier, and TapSOS, all of which attempted to solve the problem of communication.

Double majoring was not an option because of the number of units required of the deaf studies major. As a mechanical engineer, I was near my cap, and extensions were not a thing. One thing I wish I had pursued relentlessly was the double major.

To this day, I hold a fairly strong level of fluency in ASL. This is a great reminder our body language, facial expressions, and actions can speak louder than an entire opera group singing at maximum effort. Taking Gina for granted took me toward my next relationship. Gina trusted me, and I betrayed her by being unfaithful, but only confessed after being confronted after my other partner shared her interest in me with Gina.

I vowed, to myself, to remain faithful and transparent in my next relationship by disclosing intent and any loss of interest along the way.

STACEY

Stacey was someone I knew from high school for about three minutes during a game of handball, and it was her beauty that caught my attention. If time, light, quantum physics, and boiling water walked into a room, they would stop and debate who could take a second look first. The only significant comment in the three minutes we shared was she thought it was cool I had a library card hanging on my keychain.

It would be years until we spoke again. Our relationship began platonically, but that changed the more I learned about her. I was drawn by her ability to overcome the adversity of not having her father growing up and losing her mother at a young age. I admired how she overcame her struggles and went toward a medical profession. When we reconnected at CSUN, she had just gotten out of an engagement and was recovering from an abusive relationship that followed. I had just left my relationship with Gina. Neither of us were emotionally fit to be in a relationship, but I made a move anyway.

I played myself, thinking the relationship could work after telling myself it couldn't.

Part of me liked to believe it was our visions of success, advancement, wishing for a family we wanted to design for ourselves, and achieving financial independence that brought us together. However, it just wasn't the right time, and we probably were not right for one another. I take full responsibility for trying to force it to work.

When Stacey took an interest in New Student Orientation and TAKE, I recommended further consideration be given. When it came time for a summer job at a special needs camp, I made the connection hoping we would enjoy that summer working together. None of this was ever asked of me, but I knew the recommendations would be important in her development and, therefore, became important to me.

I am very grateful for realizing how far I am willing to go for those I care about when I am fully invested.

The longer Stacey and I were together, the more people would ask me if I was okay. Between my studies and our relationship, I was placing far too much time into something that was not going anywhere. I tried to prioritize my studies, but it was difficult keeping up with engineering, and that was the year I received my worst grades. I nearly failed my circuits course and missed a co-op application, which may have resulted in an internship during my fifth year at CSUN. I missed the deadline because I made Stacey my priority and forgot about others.

I played myself into thinking the relationship was important.

During the summer, the manufacturing department at CSUN would put together a course for us to have some practice with the machines. The importance of this project was getting real hands-on experience on the mills, lathes, reading engineering drawings, cutting aluminum, and having an assembly at the end. This was going to be something to show during an interview. We were making a C-clamp, which was a tool to lock something in place in a machine shop. All this tool required was a screw, frame, and handle. I rushed through the process of building the C-clamp because Stacey and I had made plans. Ultimately, the screw got stuck in the frame, which caused the screw to break in half, and there was no way to salvage the part. This broke me because I realized how much I tried to keep Stacey happy despite the extra work, as well as how I disregarded myself and my work.

That was no fault of Stacey's because I had convinced myself I could make it work. At that point, it really was only a matter of time before things ended. I was her rebound, and she was my lesson, and I could not take it anymore. My will and commitment threw in the towel from emotional exhaustion.

At the end of our relationship, Stacey asked me if I *ever actually loved her*. I remember staying silent for what felt like five minutes. I knew I did or thought it was love, but I needed to get away. So, I lied.

"I never loved you."

TODAY

A friend recently asked me if I knew what kind of love I deserved. Since 2013, I could only answer with the things I did not want from a relationship because it was much easier than to verbalize what I actually wanted. In mid-June 2021, while on my first visit to Hawaii, I was finally able to understand the type of love I deserved.

I look forward to my romantic future. Everything I do and don't do is largely based on the family I want for myself one day. When she and my children arrive, I will be ready.

Love has everything to do with my future because of the independence and time dedicated toward self-love and self-care. Only then have I been able to clearly define my priorities into a set of values that keep me centered.

1. Health, which includes physical, mental, and spiritual.
2. Career, which includes engineering, real estate, writing, and acting.
3. Community, which includes giving back to nonprofits, mentoring, and volunteering.

Learning to love taught me to love myself first.

Love has everything to do with engineering and STEM. When it comes to choosing partners, it is important to have the support necessary to achieve the impossible together. Our commencement speaker, Peggy Nelson, sector vice president of engineering and global product development at a large defense company, shared she and her first husband eventually divorced because of the lack of support when she received her first promotion to director. The union of two people is supposed to elevate what could have otherwise been accomplished alone.

My learning outcome taught me to remain alone until I find someone who meets what I want and need. To get there, heartbreak was in order.

CHAPTER 9

REFLECTIONS OF AN UNDERGRAD

—

Two hundred sixty-five rock stars, one hundred twenty-one sleepless nights, and six years of undergrad
Boy scouts have badges, and I have these numbers

My mechanical engineering degree is the fanciest receipt I now possess
I can say I am an engineer now

Being technical and learning software was important
Positioning myself for flexibility is more important

Juggling different aspects of our lives comes at a price
After my first burnout, I would do everything to prevent it

Priorities would hold me accountable
Defining values made for easy decision-making

___

As I walked the stage of commencement to shake our university president's hand, I kept thinking, *This is only the beginning. The real work begins tomorrow when I begin my big boy job.* University was a fairly sheltered time because we had a set schedule with set parameters we had to perform in. Now, I was going to be on my own with nothing but myself, the people I allowed into my circle, and my imagination.

Commencement would mean no more appointments for student advisement and no late nights studying for midterms or finals. No longer would I have to schedule my workouts at the student recreation center between group projects. It also meant I would leave my student assistant job with the Jewish Studies Department.

A part of me was going to miss all of that. The most satisfying part of the process was I made it happen for my mom and myself.

My mom came to *los Estados Unidos* with the goal of making enough money to fund her education back in Mexico. After meeting my dad, they stayed here and decided to raise us in the hope we would create a better living for ourselves. I was not going to let this wish go unfulfilled, and graduating from CSUN was my prerogative. Yes, every last minute spent studying, every energy drink I consumed, every bit of procrastination, and every group project was worth it.

As we prepared for commencement on May 18, 2015, the biggest question I had was, *Am I really prepared to go out into the working world?*

When I think about how I got here, I realize I really had no idea what I was getting into or how I was going to successfully transition out of university and into the corporate world. There was no real plan beyond finishing what my mom started in Mexico. Being first-generation meant we had to have resiliency in programming ourselves and an instinct to continuously iterate on our failures. The odds were against me, but I had several reasons to make it work, no matter how little federal or state student aid I received.

Working was the expectation, and I would work two to three part-time jobs at a time. Despite always holding down multiple jobs while studying, I had to take out additional student loans to afford myself some peace of mind.

The hardest part—getting through all the science, technology, engineering, and mathematics courses—was done with. Commencement meant my newest limitation would be what I designed for myself. Up to this point, a majority of what I did, and did not do, was expected of me. Deciding on a career path, or lack thereof, was going to be up to me.

This was where the fun began.

My greatest asset was the adversity facing a first-generation Latino born to immigrant parents of low socioeconomic status, where money and information were the limiting factors. As an adult, I refused money or information to be a limiting factor in future situations.

The two most common sayings in my Headquarters growing up were *no hay dinero* and *no gastes tu tiempo*—"there is no money" and "don't waste your time."

I was taught, like many first-generation Latinos, to have money, we had to work hard and do the jobs to get ahead.

There was a sense of impostor syndrome when I walked through my campus because I had friends who were middle-class and had defined identities as legacies of university institutions and careers they were proud of.

I could finally see something similar for myself, but I wished my family could have experienced what I was achieving with my sense of accomplishment. Culturally, this was also a series of the first positive experiences with white people that did not result in racial slurs of beaner, immigrant, wetback, or MexiCAN'T.

Achieving a 4.0 GPA in my undergrad was far less important than experiencing life as a student on campus and off campus. I was proud of being a formidable B+ student.

Between juggling several part-time jobs, on-campus student involvement, and my education, there was a high level of effort put into my engineering studies because, despite my passion, I actually struggled. Engineering school required maximum effort to retain, relearn, and perform during exams.

Physics and Strength of Materials were my most challenging courses, and I spent more time ensuring I would not have to repeat them.

Between my studies and on-campus involvement, I had to get creative with my time management. For example, during salsa practice, I would bring practice problems to solve on a whiteboard while the coaches gave us breaks. I would run through a vibrations analysis, fatigue analysis, or dynamics analysis while everyone else hung out.

When others rested, I made sure to work and do more with my time.

Fortunately, I did not have to repeat any coursework, but I was close enough where my lowest grades were a C- in both Engineering Economic Analysis and Chemistry Lab. I am by no means saying poor grades are okay, but I am saying some poor grades will not dampen graduation. All the extra effort was worth it, and I was happy to finish my undergrad with a 3.26 GPA.

The untold story in the GPA is the adversity I had to overcome and the tenacity required to do it.

Actually, I do have a confession: I failed one course.

I took a calculus course at Santa Monica Community College to try to stay ahead of the coursework, but my professor was tough on his students. I failed the first two quizzes and first midterm, so I checked out of the course and simply took the F. Since it was at Santa Monica Community College, those units would never transfer over to affect my CSUN GPA or coursework. If I had passed, great. If I failed or stopped attending class, it was like it never happened.

Confession number two; I failed my Fundamentals of Engineering (FE) exam for my Engineering in Training (EIT) licensing twice before passing.

I took that exam in October 2013 at the Pomona Fair Complex in Pomona, CA, confident I could figure out most of the exam questions via the process of elimination. The exam was multiple choice, and we had a reference manual to use at our discretion. My confidence got the best of me and backfired. My second attempt was in March 2016 at a testing center in Pasadena. The biggest difference was I was actively studying, but I would fall short on a majority of the topics. On my third attempt, I went in with the mindset my livelihood depended on this exam. My studying was relentless during my breaks at work, my off-time from work, and weekends.

I was overly confident in the first two attempts. Putting in the time to study was necessary to pass. Passing meant I belonged to a group of first-generation Latinos who pursued higher education and were working toward receiving professional licensing. This would be an additional tool on my résumé.

BURNOUT

"Earning an engineering degree was the easiest milestone ever!" said nobody ever.

I do not regret my choice of major, but I do wish I had prepared myself better for the mind-numbing amount of study required for the major. I began my undergrad overly confident in my abilities to earn good grades. The first few months, I did not attend class when I didn't have to and would count on my memory to get me through tests and quizzes.

I figured, *This was how I got through high school, so it should be the same here.* Wow, was I wrong!

Engineering required immense amounts of dedicated study and continued practice. Engineering was not intuitive for me. I was comfortable with math and science, but I struggled to put all the concepts together. Drilling problems was the only way to build an aptitude and mastery of the subjects.

Professors held high expectations of each student. Our group assignments were no exception to this rule. It often felt as if the formulas and principles had to become a part of my psyche for me to fully understand.

Progressing through the coursework required the principles from the previous semester be inherited and become second nature, like breathing. At the start of most semesters, we would review problems from a previous course to make certain we had the fundamentals secured. This was the biggest hurdle in being a STEM major. Cruising through one course would force us to make it all up in the next.

I was not a terrible student, but I was not a great one either. I found greater satisfaction in being involved on campus. Therefore, I was often drawn to the events and groups outside of engineering. When it came down to it, I considered myself a B+ student but made certain to be an A+ citizen on campus.

Beyond my studies, I had my work-study with the Jewish Studies Interdisciplinary Studies department, part-time work mentoring, boxing, the Salsa Libre dance team practices, intramural sports, Sigma Lambda Beta International

Fraternity Incorporated, the Society of Hispanic Professional Engineers (SHPE), Hermanos Unidos (HU), and New Student Orientation (NSO), all while trying to keep my grades alive.

Extreme involvement was an understatement. I was *becoming* the CSUN campus.

Being the first in my family to attend university, I wanted to experience everything I could as fast as possible. I'd eventually find that was unsustainable and eventually paid the price with burnout.

Burnout feels a lot like food poisoning, at least the part where you don't want to do anything except lie in bed and stare at the ceiling because of the mental exhaustion, devoid of motivation. The only thing I wanted to do when I experienced burnout was lie in bed and be a *cobija*. Every waking moment was stressful. I felt like I was drowning in an ocean of responsibility I created for myself, and there was an anchor tied to both my feet while I tried to tread water.

Spring 2013 was when I experienced my first burnout—oh, yes, this happened more than once. There was a second incident, but the first is always the worst. My priorities were nonexistent and misaligned to anything other than experiencing as much as I could as fast as possible. I managed to get a lot done, but that is miserable when the fun is sucked out of it.

The clearest sign of experiencing burnout was my sleeping patterns. Almost every location you could think of became a place to nap, including bathroom stalls, my car, the library, lectures, meetings, and dates. I basically transformed into a cat. Naps are very effective tools, but naps do not and will not replace quality sleep. The other signs were irritability and loss of focus from simple tasks, like responding to or drafting an email.

Wanting to experience as much as possible in my time in undergrad was a large motivator, but this behavior also came from a fear of failure. I was proud of being able to pull off all-nighters studying and say "yes" to everything. Being able to get things done was a badge of honor, but at what price?

In my mind, if I was able to juggle as much as I did during undergrad, then I would surely be able to do the same when I finished with undergrad. My biggest role model was my mom.

My mom raised three children, went to work, completed household duties, and remained involved in our schooling—she was a superhero! I never took notice of or heard her complaining about the hard work or being tired ever. That gave me the impression it was effortless.

Had I not learned my lesson during undergrad, there would have been a constant theme of burnout in my professional work, where I was likely to feel like a slave to my own work ethic.

I had no boundaries in undergrad. I was willing, able, and ready to say "yes" to anything that crossed my path. When it came to supporting a greater good, I was all in. The women in STEM community group? Count me in. The LGBTQ community? Count me in. The new salsa dancers? Count me in.

Although these were synonymous with bits of myself and friends, there was no prioritization by saying "yes" to any of it.

To maximize my time remaining involved, I would take my homework with me wherever I went. If I was at a salsa dancing social, I was cranking out problems between my rest periods of intensive dancing. If I was at a community equality rally, I was reviewing my notes on my phone from the pictures I had taken.

If there is one bit of advice I would give my twenty-one-year-old self in 2013, it would be to have clear boundaries to avoid burnout. If left untreated, burnout can lead to a continued pattern of an "evolution from pressured, overscheduled, college-résumé-building children to exhausted, overworked, LinkedIn-building adults" (Meyer, 2020).

When I began to prioritize my values, it was from the perspective of the first incident of burnout. If there was going to be any longevity in my plan to pursue several careers in parallel, there had to be self-discipline. I made a commitment to myself that work would not come before health, and being involved in extracurricular activities was an added incentive for accomplishing what was necessary in my regular duties in engineering, real estate, investing, and writing.

My values and priorities have evolved in the last eight years to reflect my focus. In this order:

- Health
- Career
- Community

If I learned anything from burning out, it's going too fast will slow you down. As much as I'd like to think I am invincible, I am not. Taking care of my health means I am doing well in mind, body, and spirit. Balancing my careers means I am doing well in engineering, real estate, investing, and writing, where the realization there is no multicareer portfolio without a healthy engineer.

Only after these first two are taken care of can I comfortably engage with my community. Community is important, but it cannot be more important than my wellbeing.

The manner in which I do everything I do is to prevent burnout. There will be days when more effort is required, but this is meticulously engineered effort I know about in advance as opposed to spontaneously requiring it from me.

This is the perfect combination of the Mamba mentality, coined by Kobe Bryant, where we become the best versions of ourselves and prepare ourselves for success in the process. I found this makes for a much more satisfying and less overwhelming life.

SEEKING EMPLOYMENT

Finding my first job out of university was difficult without any formal engineering experience or internship at some fancy company. All I had to show were my student projects. However, those student projects turned out to be far more valuable than I had ever imagined they would be when presented to the right people. Student projects and leveraging my engineering network with the different sponsors in my corner were more than enough to earn me my first shot.

The 2014–2015 academic year was one of the most deliberative grinds I had to muster. As president to the Society of Hispanic Professional Engineers (SHPE) at CSUN chapter, I felt an added responsibility to establish a benchmark for first-generation Latinos, like me, to empower themselves and those in the periphery. Ours began as a dying chapter, and I wanted to reestablish a once nationally award-winning chapter because of the impact the members who came before did for me.

Our membership was low, and it was both my goal and our duty as board members to revive the chapter and make sure it was on a course to sustain itself over an extended number of years.

As I write this now, in 2021, the CSUN SHPE chapter continues to flourish.

My passion and gratitude for SHPE stems from helping me and my peers be better prepared for the corporate world by providing the resources of mentorship, professional development, and career readiness. It was here I learned having a great résumé with the right descriptions is not enough if our character and interpersonal skills didn't complement the piece of paper. Interviewing, personal branding, public speaking, and networking are important skills to practice well before graduation.

Every year, SHPE hosts its signature event, the National Conference, where employers seek talent to hire into their organizations for internships and full-time roles. It was my goal to attend during my last year at CSUN. I interviewed with GE Aviation, Aerotek, and Honeywell, but nothing came of those interviews. I left the conference slightly discouraged from not receiving an offer, but with invaluable practice that would set me up for success.

There was also the Nissan Design Competition I participated in, where we were split into different groups and tasked with delivering a solution to a sustainability project in an effort to conserve water in developing countries. Our group was a runner-up in the competition, where we pitched our idea to a panel of industry professionals.

After I returned from the conference, my search for a full-time job was much more focused because I refused to move back to Headquarters after graduation. From SHPE, I learned applying online would do very little for me, so I consulted my sphere of influence and network for referrals.

From there, I interviewed with San Diego Gas & Electric, SoCalGas, and Mason Electric. I realized my prospects for industries of interest were all over the place, but as a first-generation Latino leaving university, finding any work was more important than finding work I wanted to do. In fact, I gave very little consideration to the industry because they all interested me, and I knew I could perform well in any of them. As fate would have it, I would join Mason Electric the day after graduation as a mechanical design engineer.

Despite being an engineer, perfection was not high on my list of priorities. Having a fundamental understanding of the subject matter was much more important, and I knew that understanding could take me further than my GPA ever could.

Never did I allow my GPA to define what I could or could not do because telling my story was up to me. Iterating my story and making sure I gave myself permission to fail and experiment got me to where I am.

Pursuing an engineering degree was almost masochistic because of all the mental processing power required for the material and theory. If I was presented with the question, "If you could pursue a completely different major, what major would that be?" I would most definitely *not* change my major. Learning about engineering through math and science was fun, and it really opened up my imagination to the possibilities of the world. A STEM degree prepares you to think differently while refining your interpersonal skills and testing your limitations of time management, mental health, and being able to graduate.

There are a lot of stereotypes associated with majoring in and working as an engineer. We are nerds. We only love to study and not do anything fun. We take life too seriously. Guess what, we are many, and we are mighty, so much so we can study for two hours with the efficiency of five hours and still make time for a Bad Bunny or Maluma concert.

Thank you, STEM, because you taught me everything I didn't know I needed to.

As I proceeded to shake the president's hand at commencement, I kept thinking, *Please don't trip as you walk the stage, but if you do, make sure it's the most graceful fall, so you make a lasting impression.*

STAGE THREE

PARADIGM TRANSPOSITION

CHAPTER 10

THE DAY AFTER GRADUATION

———

This was my American dream
Employment the day after finishing undergrad

I locked in my first big kid job as a design engineer
Six years of engineering school was worth it

I strongly believed my engineering education was relevant
It was not what I imagined

By my own definition, I achieved the first-generation dream—
securing employment to go to the day after graduation.

I graduated on May 18, 2015, and had work waiting for me
on May 19, 2015, as a design engineer. Before I agreed to go
straight to work after graduation, my supervisor emphasized
it was okay for me to take a few days for myself. I thanked
him for the consideration, but I was eager to get started.

The lingering thought of a break honestly gave me anxiety. I wanted to make the impression I would be hardworking and ready for anything.

I could not get any sleep the night before. The anxiety and stress from trying to find employment evolved into hope and excitement after securing it. I was revisiting and reviewing the advice from commencement day.

Our commencement speaker was Peggy Nelson, sector vice president of engineering and global product development at a large defense company, who shared six things for us to remember:

- Have great assignments.
- Ethics is where it's at.
- Execute on priorities.
- Earn the right sponsors.
- Choose the right partner.
- Live life with the right passion.

As I sat in my cap and gown, dripping in purple, white, blue, and black sashes with orange, red, and white chords, I made sure to pay attention to every last lesson learned. During her speech, the first piece of advice that struck me was her emphasis on following the money and encouraging us to do so. She had said:

"I don't mean to follow where you are going to get the highest salary. That is not what I mean by following the money. What I do mean is to follow how the company makes a profit in your assignments. Find tough, messy cleanup assignments in the area where the company makes its sales."

Before that event, I did not consider how sales, profit, and engineering meshed together, but I learned they have everything to do with each other.

Bottom line: there is no engineering organization without any sales and profit irrespective of whether the company sells products and services.

I figured, somewhere along my way, I would need sales experience. Large, medium, small, and startup enterprises exist to deliver a service or product, solving some problem a customer has. Every producer of a product needs engineers to design, maintain, improve, and innovate existing and new products.

Cleanup assignments caught my interest because they meant we would not have to begin with a clean slate, and instead, we could improve on a product, service, or process. This required seeing value where no one else did, like finding hidden treasure. Finding the opportunity, I could see myself building a career from cleaning up the messy stuff because I could give an additional perspective as a first-generation person of color.

Most of us want the glory without having to delve into an abyss of a project. Cleaning up a mess means becoming immersed in the problems of others while maintaining sanity, and I was okay with that. Call me a glutton for punishment, but I am okay with the difficult conversations, negotiations, compromise, sleepless nights, and creative problem-solving.

This thrill either makes me a project junkie or CEO in the making.

Peggy Nelson made sure to engage us during her delivery with thought-provoking statements like:

"Show of hands, how many of you think your boss is going to become your new most important person? How many think your peers will be your most important group at work? How about the people who may work for you? Look to your right and the people who are sitting right next to you. Yes, your bosses and your employees are clearly important, but your peers have a nasty way of becoming your boss."

In another example, Peggy shared being part of a twenty-person management development team working on a strategic initiative. Of the group, 90 percent of them became executives, and one of them would later become the CEO of the company. He was the same person who promoted Peggy to vice president. Her key takeaway was, "Where do you think I would be if, seven years into my career, I had been nasty to that particular peer? It's important to remember as you navigate your career that mentors will give you sage advice, but a sponsor uses their leverage and reputation to get you the right job and opportunity to prove yourself."

From this, an important practice of remaining equal and fair to peers and collaborators would prove to be essential to any and all future endeavors. Who knows when a CEO in the making is in the same room.

This was the most excited I had been since I signed my offer letter two weeks earlier in Burbank, CA. I submitted upward of 371 job applications, interviewed for ten different roles, and I was overcaffeinated. Toward the end of my search for employment, it was nice to have options between cosmetics, utilities, and manufacturing, though I chose manufacturing because I could see this position would take me into aerospace and defense. Not receiving an offer from one of the large three defense contractors just meant I had to take a detour. I knew the messy assignments, difficult conversations, and growth were waiting for me.

This manufacturing company was dedicated to making control systems and switches for fixed wing aircraft, rotary aircraft, ground vehicles, and naval platforms. The best way to describe it was they designed the interface between man and machine in a cockpit for the prime defense contractors. They had an impressive portfolio built in their sixty-five years of service. That was the first time I would see the technology our war fighters would interface with and was the added purpose I needed.

Three hours of sleep was all I got that night, but it didn't matter. I had a job to go to and a world full of possibilities. I was ready for whatever it took to succeed. Overtime, late nights, projects nobody wanted, traveling, and collaborating with other engineers—I was ready for it all.

One thing I wish I knew sooner was that this first role would not be glamorous. It sounded great on paper, and the website showed great things, but my actual assignment was not the most exciting. I was a paper-pusher, but it taught me to switch my perspective and see beyond my current circumstances and to the opportunities that may be bestowed from that single experience.

There were new aspects of engineering—aside from sales and profit learned during commencement—I did not consider, like supply chain, shipping and handling, contracts, and compliance. This was a benchmark for the work I wanted and the mindset I needed to set me off in a multidisciplinary environment.

I made the realization maybe this was something a CEO would one day want me to know. It was not clear then, but it helped set a path for everything else I would eventually do.

The morning of May 19, I got onto my Kawasaki Ninja 250R and made sure to arrive extra early. It was obvious I had arrived too early because I had to wait for the receptionist to open the door.

While I waited about ten minutes for my new badge, I must have seen two dozen other colleagues pass me by. The company had about five hundred employees—a mix of engineers, sales, manufacturing, testing, customer service, and export compliance.

Export compliance was going to be like a second Headquarters for the next year and a half. I just did not know it yet.

After receiving my badge, I was escorted into my supervisor's office to receive my assignment, tour the company, and make introductions. The next two weeks were a combination of training and becoming familiar with the company's products and services. I was not expected to know everything, but I made sure to ask any questions I had, no matter how repetitive they were. Learning was an expectation, and I wanted the organization to know there was not going to be a task too small or too large for my due diligence.

My supervisor placed a strong emphasis on my attitude and willingness to learn as a big reason for bringing me onboard, where intelligence could be found in many engineers who had interviewed.

My manager was a positive, supportive, and strategic man. This put me at ease because I felt comfortable asking questions and help, and yes, it also put me at ease knowing he was someone of color. One of the first questions I asked him was about the biggest lesson or piece of advice he wished he had learned early in his career.

The story he had for me was regarding a customer experience where they questioned a quote he had delivered for products they needed. When he reported back to his supervisor to share the news, he was relieved his leadership supported him on his delivery. He had done everything right, and his supervisor acknowledged this. The takeaway for me was if we trusted we had done everything we could correctly, all would be well.

Most engineers grow up fantasizing about building something as cool as an Iron Man suit or some fancy plane that goes supersonic speeds, but not me. My engineering fantasies would not come until after I left undergrad. Growing up, I bounced between the idea of being a teacher, a police officer, and a scientist. A scientist was fairly close to engineering, but the biggest distinction was engineers were the ones making the ideas of the scientist come to life.

My engineering fantasy was being able to work on cutting-edge technologies that progress the safety and livelihood of people on Earth. It's far more important to care for the planet we have and extend its life.

What I knew for certain was I wanted to have a job that was interesting and paid decently to save as much money as possible and avoid struggling with finances like my parents did. It was this mindset that helped me get out of twenty-three thousand dollars in student loan debt in one year by living a college student lifestyle after finishing undergrad.

Majoring as a mechanical engineer meant we cared about how systems and parts could fail. Understanding the different failure modes—vibration, torsion, bending, compression, tension, fatigue, humidity, and corrosion—and knowing how to decide where the failures happen and under what circumstances are parts of the process. In my eyes, design and life were not much different. Failure was inevitable, and we must iterate to have a favorable outcome, just as we would with products. This was the level of analysis I thought was required at my design engineer job.

As I learned, there was analysis, but not the type undergrad prepared me for.

In my dream world, I would utilize CAD software to design and create failure simulations, use mathematical models to determine how failure may occur, and display it all on a screen with pretty colors for our control systems. Export Compliance required, what I imagine lawyers needed to know, the ability to read through logic to arrive at a conclusion of guilty or not guilty, with evidence to back it up.

I was consumed by this new unfamiliar world of shipping products and the licensing to comply with national and international regulations.

Export Compliance required we make sure shipped products within the continental United States (CONUS) or outside the continental United States (OCONUS) were assigned the appropriate codes for tax, security, and census purposes. The objective was to make sure advanced and protected technologies did not accidentally arrive at destinations they were not supposed to go. I learned about all sorts of programs I would not have otherwise known about. I'd also learned shipments confiscated or reviewed by US Customs and Border Protection was something that could halt an entire supply chain—locally and globally.

Every product entering and leaving our borders needed to be assigned the proper codes, or else they would be confiscated for failing to comply with the Export Administration Regulations (EAR). In the most serious cases, failure to comply could result in fines, jail time, and delayed shipments, which directly impact customer relationships and company sales.

The usefulness of an engineering education was in determining the different applications of products and their material compositions; understanding their assemblies; and recognizing where modifications to form, fit, and function constitute specially designed versus the dreaded specifically designed, as defined by the United States Munitions List (USML). This was all new legal jargon to me, but it was essential to completing our statement of work (SOW).

After we got through an analysis, we determined whether a product required a license to export because our management, customers, and the government wanted to know. It would take weeks to get the appropriate licenses. The highest level of export is a "ITAR controlled product," which is determined per the International Traffic in Arms Regulations (ITAR). In a nutshell, these are products that need to have extremely careful handling when shipped and can only be shipped in specific conditions.

Staying out of jail and delivering my best work was important, so I made sure to disclose if an item was governed by ITAR or speculated to be governed accordingly. There was a lot of learning involved, and I made sure to ask lots of questions.

My proficiency was well enough to eventually teach export compliance to about sixty mid- and senior-level engineers at the company. That was a proud moment for this first-gen Latino. After all, if we consider the overhead from this one training, it was valued at tens of thousands of dollars, accounting for hourly wages and overhead.

Our team was small, and our SOW was large. Luckily, I had training from the finest in the company. We were the Fantastic Four, the tiger team, the export classification team. I loved my team. We had an entire war room dedicated to export classification, making it that much more important and one of the messy projects Peggy was talking about.

From what I know now, had my experience been strictly engineering, my time would have been miserable. I figured out senior year in undergrad that technical work was not my calling after I was offered the chief engineering role for our senior design project. This was a flattering phone call with Professor Khachatourians.

It was during this same call my professor emphasized, "Being a great engineer does not mean being the most technical. In fact, some of the greatest leaders in an organization are not the most technical. Instead, they rely on groups of individuals to help them navigate the technical work. This is what I see from you!" The other realization there was understanding that I really loved working with and developing people. I chose the presidency for the Society of Hispanic Professional Engineers'(SHPE) CSUN chapter in place of chief engineer for senior design.

The proudest moment at the manufacturing company was supporting the development of systems to lighten our load. In our arsenal was a computer programming wizard who automated much of the documentation we needed for each analysis. With a careful organization of servers, several documents, and a click of a button, we would sort through thousands of lines of data and generate a preliminary package for our review.

The primary document in the package was the equivalent of a survey that followed a series of questions identifying the use and composition and supporting documentation for our analysis. Our analysis could be anywhere from four to twenty-plus pages. This was a great lesson in engineering: when data is involved, automate!

I am by no means a programming wizard, nor do I hold an interest in being so, but I recognize and respect the art and those who practice and navigate the complexity. Throughout my career, I would learn to build good relationships with these groups because there is instant value-added from their contributions and projects they may eagerly be waiting for. I identified them as the engineering wizard, which was a value I would otherwise not be able to bring.

Our work had no end, and the more product we shipped, the more analysis was required. Senior-level engineers would call this job security, and although it was a comforting thought, the work was too predictable to be satisfying. I needed a dynamic environment of volatility, uncertainty, complexity, and ambiguity where I could interact with more people in the organization. Although I knew that was not where I would remain in the long term, I treated it like it was so my performance would not be impaired.

There were days where I would look at the clock and watch the second hand make its way slowly about the clock face. These were the tougher days. I doubted if engineering was the right choice. I questioned whether I was the only one with these feelings of frustration, unfulfillment, and dissatisfaction, but I would later learn I was not the only one.

My biggest conflict was this feeling seemed like a betrayal to the gratitude I felt of having a career to begin with the day after graduation.

When I asked for tougher assignments, I was heard but never listened to, and the request was never fulfilled. As soon as I made this request, I was back in the war room doing export compliance. I took the responsibility to seek those tougher assignments internally before I decided to move on from export compliance. About a year and a half later, my search would take me to a much larger organization that would challenge my aptitude and provide the engineering problems I would be excited to solve. It was there I would continue to learn about the meaning of defining possible.

CHAPTER 11

STUDENT LOANS FINANCED MY FUTURE

———

My parents taught me debt was bad
None of them had credit and insisted on paying cash

I adopted those beliefs
Then student loans afforded me an education

Student loan financing changed everything
My world changed, realizing the power of debt

Debt can be managed as a strategic vehicle
I began riding on the HOV lane toward success

My parents' advice on money was similar to most first-generation Latino households, *trabaja duro y no tengas deudas para poder guardar todo el dinero que puedas.* This was my foundation for any financial strategy I had after graduation, but first, I had to take care of the twenty-three thousand dollars in student loans. Now that I had a big boy job that paid forty-eight thousand dollars a year, after taxes, with benefits and a retirement plan, I could create a financial strategy toward some obscure version of first-generation wealth.

For a kid growing up in East Hollywood, a salary of forty-eight thousand a year was a huge jump from the thirteen thousand I was earning from all my part-time jobs as a student. This was nearly four times those earnings.

A majority of my earnings were allocated to paying down those student loans. To keep me motivated, I reminded myself with a vision board I created that included peace of mind, increasing wealth, satisfaction from pursuing several careers, and establishing a family of my own.

For my student loans to be paid off, my studentlike lifestyle didn't change for two years. The biggest obstacle was being disciplined enough to defer travel plans from invitations to go to Hawaii, China, Spain, France, Brazil, and Canada. There was nothing more exciting than being able to explore the unknown, but I had to remain strong and focused. I knew these destinations were likely not going anywhere, which was how I was able to say "no." To relieve any curiosity, I spent time on YouTube to witness the many things I could expect to see on future trips to these places.

The same roommates I had my senior year in undergrad were who I lived with in my two years after graduating. This was the same house in Northridge on Superior Street. I also continued driving my red Kawasaki Ninja 250R to get everywhere, deferring the purchase of a new or lightly used vehicle for a later time. The most extravagant purchases I allowed myself to make were a new laptop that I continued to use six years later and my Nikon DSLR.

All my meals were prepped like a good gym rat to encourage a healthy lifestyle. Staying healthy also meant I would bypass having to visit the doctor, dentist, or optometrist for anything other than routine physicals, cleanings, and prescription updates. Very little thought went into the creation of this plan since I lived this reality. By far, the most rewarding outcome besides bringing a debt to zero was the continued self-discipline to make sure I did not make any unreasonable decisions.

For the sake of accuracy, I logged onto my student loan provider portal, Great Lakes, on January 15, 2021, to have a better idea of what my financial obligation looked like. I was equally curious about what my thought process may have been at ages seventeen through twenty-two. Below is the outline of the student loans and their interest rates I accepted at the beginning of each academic year when FAFSA would ask if I wanted to accept these loans.

There are important distinctions between the two types of loans offered by the Great Lakes provider: subsidized and unsubsidized loans. The big difference is during a deferment period. Unsubsidized loans will continue to accrue interest, while subsidized will not. The prefix "-un" gives the impression this would be the better of the two, but it isn't. Our high school college counselor had drilled this into us, and it stayed engraved in my mind.

Thank you, Mrs. Campbell!

In no way do I undermine my intelligence in navigating these early financial decisions, but I am definitely surprised by how much thought went into my decision-making.

- Age seventeen | Year 2009 | Direct Subsidized Stafford Loan | $3,023 Loan | 5.600 percent Fixed Interest
- Age eighteen | Year 2010 | Direct Subsidized Stafford Loan | $3,500 Loan | 4.500 percent Fixed Interest
- Age nineteen | Year 2011 | Direct Subsidized Stafford Loan | $4,500 Loan | 3.400 percent Fixed Interest
- Age twenty | Year 2012 | Direct Subsidized Stafford Loan | $2,500 Loan | 3.400 percent Fixed Interest
- Age twenty-one | Year 2013 | Direct Subsidized Stafford Loan | $4,500 Loan | 3.860 percent Fixed Interest
- Age twenty-two | Year 2014 | Direct Subsidized Stafford Loan | $4,977 Loan | 4.660 percent Fixed Interest

When I accepted these loans, I did not consult my parents. How could I? Neither of them had credit or loans. I knew they would immediately advise me not to take them. Knowing this, I will admit my decision to accept the loan my first year was impulsive with the justification I was going to college so I could pay it off later. The second year, it was out of need. Living away from home was expensive. The expenses I knew I was going to have—rent, utilities, books, groceries, insurance, and outings—added up.

Had I not had my student assistant job at the beginning of my second year at CSUN, I would have really been in trouble. Not only was my student assistant job convenient by being on campus, but I was in a favorable position because of work-study. Having a work-study grant made me competitive to the department because it was money the department saved.

I nearly lost my work-study grant by not knowing what it was. I remember receiving an email from the GE Honors program office about an opening with the Jewish Studies Department as a student assistant to the department chair. I arrived late to my interview, drenched in sweat. I had no real good excuse other than waking up late.

Had it been me holding the interview, I would have dismissed the candidate. Jody, my supervisor, was a blessing the five years I was able to work with and for her.

Between securing on-campus employment and having a great supervisor, I was extremely fortunate in my years in undergrad. Thinking back, I probably don't give myself enough credit for my reasoning in financial decisions.

I'm proud of the twenty-three-year-old version of me for being acquainted with the words "capitalization," "deferment," "forbearance," "subsidized," and "unsubsidized." Before I began my student loan payments sometime in late 2016, I used my deferment allowance to increase my savings for the added peace of mind should my motorcycle need repairs or new tires, I faced a medical emergency, or any other unforeseen circumstance happened.

For many of us first-generation persons of color, financing or paying for higher education is the starting point to building wealth, and we take that chance on ourselves. For many of us, that is the beginning, leading us to the next step, like investing.

I realized the value of delayed gratification from paying off my student loans and seeing how twenty-three thousand was a lot of money, but at the same time, this was within reach. The next step was to become an active investor.

In May of 2016, I opened up my stock trading account with TD Ameritrade. This was before it was cool to invest on apps like Robinhood, Acorns, or Webull, and every trade was commission-free. My portfolio began with thirteen hundred dollars toward stock trading. One year after I opened my account, the value doubled. The following year, I doubled it again.

This would become my nest egg toward my first real estate purchase, real estate rental, and commission check. One of the benefits of becoming licensed, and a distinguishing perk to someone unlicensed, is collecting commissions on a sale after the Escrow closes. It was a four-in-one deal that required long-term thinking and believing in the possibility of realizing flexible outcomes.

The inspiration to trade stocks came from my coworkers at the first engineering company I was hired onto since they would always talk about "the market" and the hottest technologies that might reap them large returns. We were engineers, so it felt natural to be hyped by technology. They were much older and had houses, vacation homes, and portfolios they proudly talked about during breaks.

I wanted to be a part of these conversations, so I got started with whatever the minimum amount was at the time to create an account. Seeing them get excited and hearing them talk about the future made me excited. Knowing little to nothing was not enough to make me shy away from investing. I grew up believing the fallacy that only the wealthy traded stocks.

When I was researching different brokers, I made sure they had educational tools and platforms I could use to learn the art of trading. I would spend hours at night on the Ameritrade Education Center and Lynda.com, present-day LinkedIn Learning, to become familiar with the fundamentals, which boiled down to understanding financial statements and extracting valuations based on the organizations of interest future or lack thereof. Along with this excursion of study, I became better acquainted with my risk tolerance and the risks associated with investing. Due diligence was something I was already accustomed to from my engineering, so ascertaining to this requirement was effortless.

Up to that point, financial literacy also meant knowing what I was going to sign. No longer was I the seventeen-year-old who took what he was offered under the premise it could be paid off later. There would be extensive market research and timeliness in the decision-making.

Perhaps the greatest financial advice I learned during my undergrad was from Jody on not making financial decisions after seven o'clock at night because that could lead to very poor, emotional decisions. Lack of self-discipline could mean spiraling into a world of never-ending debt and back into the low socioeconomic status I was consciously trying to get away from.

Do I regret taking those student loans? Not at all, but I do wish I had taken scholarships and grants more seriously. Twenty-three thousand was a lot of money at the time. The numbers worked out after graduation since I had plenty of residual income living the same college student lifestyle. Living below my means, keeping a reasonably healthy lifestyle, and saving worked!

I continue to practice these principles to this day. The greatest lesson those student loans taught me was not about the six years of education but the financial responsibility and literacy I forced myself to have after leaving undergrad because adulting is expensive! Paying off 2,300,000 pennies in student loans forced me into financial literacy.

My student loans were fully paid off on December 12, 2017. Go, me!

CSUN was a great financial accident. Paying Sallie Mae back trained me to be ready for investing and developing my master plan toward creating my version of wealth, which continues with education.

I flirted with the idea of pursuing a master's through undergrad. Toward the end of my undergrad, I started having second thoughts because of the price tag and advice from SHPE guest speakers who spoke on their experiences. Common advice was coming out of undergrad. We really don't have an idea of what it is we want to do. Taking a few years to try out different roles would make the decision-making much easier. And that is exactly what I did.

I told myself I should first get some work experience and have a taste of different roles before deciding what my focus for a master's degree could be. The hard deadline I gave myself was by age thirty. I would have completed a master's, which gave me a five-year cushion to figure out what I wanted to do. Funding my education post-undergrad would be an out-of-pocket expense unless I found an organization that believed in investing in their employees and would sponsor my education.

One of the many perks of having STEM-based employment is the benefit of educational assistance and, in certain situations, fully funded assistance. This was a highlight by many guest speakers I observed. I was determined to find this unicorn. Experiencing undergrad and not having criteria inspired me to create my own requirements for a master's. In my search, I had four very clear, nonnegotiable requirements:

1. The program shall be on the subject of systems engineering with coursework and emphasis on business development or management.
2. The program shall be fully funded by my employer.
3. The program shall facilitate my transition into a different engineering role as a promotion.
4. The program shall not be any longer than a year and a half to complete and must be recognized as a master's degree, not a certificate.

Deferring my decision to pursue my master's was brilliant. By deferring my education, I allowed myself to experience what the work environment, work dynamics, and global trend in the workforce looked like. The more honest reason was I was not willing to compromise my budget.

Some engineering-based programs in systems engineering were at least twenty thousand dollars for a two-year, full-time program, and I was not about to take time off work. I was skeptical about my last requirement on the length of time to complete. Time was becoming more essential than dollars.

Being more financially literate, I felt responsible to act accordingly. The thought process went something like this:

1. Having financial support would lessen the financial burden. I was okay with a contingency where I had to serve time with the company. Otherwise, I would have to pay the sponsorship back for leaving the company before the agreed contingency period of service.
2. Having a master's could potentially open up negotiations for a promotion and salary increase, internally and externally.
3. I was not okay with spending more time in school than necessary. Time became a new form of currency.

I found my unicorn meeting all of the criteria in a city I told myself I would one day live and own real estate. The University of California San Diego (UCSD) offered a yearlong program in Architecture-based Enterprise Systems Engineering (AESE), which was designed for the full-time professional.

This was an in-class program that required I be at UCSD on the scheduled class dates.

To meet the in-class instruction requirement, I would stay near UCSD for two to four straight days to be an active participant and make a 360-mile roundtrip on those weeks class was in session. Making the commute was a small price to pay considering the program was fully funded, valued at thirty-three thousand dollars for the year, and only required my presence on my Fridays off and the following weekends.

Yes, the commute was brutal. I timed my departure from Palmdale so I could avoid LA County and Orange County traffic in the direction of San Diego. Ample time for traffic and rest was essential because I did not want to be a hazard to anyone on the road. When necessary, I pulled into a parking lot, usually a Target or Costco, to rest my eyes and power-nap for eleven minutes.

Power naps worked every time.

On my first two school sessions, I booked hotels, which then evolved into staying with friends, and then into sleeping in my burgundy 1996 Saturn SL1 at a rest area before entering San Diego. Hotels were expensive, and friends had lives to live, and I did not want to overstay my welcome. For most of my schooling at UCSD, I slept in my car at the Aliso Creek Rest Area right before arriving in Oceanside. I also took advantage of my 24 Hour Fitness gym membership to shower. I was up by 4:30 a.m. to drive the remaining thirty minutes to work out, get dressed, and make my way to class. I thought this was genius!

Credit has to be given to a podcast I once listened to about being homeless, where a guest said if he was ever homeless, the first purchase he would make would be a gym membership for the accessibility to fitness and grooming.

Had I needed a hotel for longer than the five hours of sleep I was going to get at a rate of one hundred fifty dollars a night, then it may have made sense. Paying thirty dollars an hour to sleep did not make any sense to me.

Two years after paying off my student loans, I was still living the student lifestyle. Part of the financial journey was to keep as much of my take-home pay to work for me through investments.

If I did not see value in my education, I would have stopped believing student loans financed my education. Instead, student loans financed my future by evolving my mindset and discipline in handling money. CSUN was not my first choice, but it was the best choice and probably the only choice to have achieved this evolution.

CHAPTER 12

TOASTMASTERS DISTRICT 52 COMPETITION

———

Anxiety from public speaking does not disappear
The anxiety just hits a little different with experience

Once upon a time, I had anxiety
It began an entire month leading up to a speaking event

A month evolved into a week
A week into a day

Days became seconds
With this discipline, my peak of public speaking was
competition

———

Twenty-five percent of Americans fear public speaking over heights, drowning, blood, flying, and zombies (Ingraham, 2014). Once upon a time, I belonged to that demographic. My fear was so overwhelming I'd be on a public bus sweating out of fear someone might talk to me in public. I was fifteen.

What if I say the wrong thing? What if I can't think of anything to say? What if I'm not interesting enough? I psyched myself out over the thought of actually having a conversation. Most of this fear came from a lack of confidence.

The ages of eleven through sixteen were the most difficult when it came to speaking publicly. I was short, overweight, and looked like pizza. I was not happy with my appearance, where the only factor I had control over was my weight. Puberty hit me hard, which is why I looked like pizza. There came a turning point where I was fed up with being shy and unable to have the confidence to speak up.

Practice during my late teens took the form of regular participation in class, volunteering, taking on leadership roles, and attending more social events. Eventually, my practice became more purposeful and calculated.

The first time I ever heard about Toastmasters was during undergrad. Several of my mentors and role models belonging to the Society of Hispanic Professional Engineers (SHPE) were Toastmasters and spoke highly of the organization. From context, I poked fun at the name by saying it was an organization dedicated to the mastery of toasting bread.

Toastmasters is an educational nonprofit organization dedicated to teaching the art of public speaking and leadership. So, not only were these accomplished STEM professionals contributing to the community by volunteering, but they were also developing themselves into even more polished speakers. The self-improvement paid off because when one of these speakers went on stage, they commanded the room with conviction and charisma, which I thought was otherworldly for engineers.

It turns out, public speaking is a superpower engineer—and frankly anybody—is able to attain, sustain, and share with the world. Anyone with a yearning to be heard and share their thoughts is able to master it with practice.

STEM professionals must regularly communicate to advance project milestones, engage customers, deliberate with team members, create cohesion at the office, and solve problems. Communication and presentation skills are intangible assets that will not diminish in value. Having an aptitude for communication meant there was greater mobility working between individuals or in team settings. Making ideas as simple as possible while keeping an audience engaged is an art. Seeing my SHPE professional role models succeed made me realize I should work toward becoming a more proficient public speaker.

After I finished my undergraduate, I became a member of Toastmasters in August of 2015. After my first meeting as a guest, I knew I had to be a part of this organization. Disclaimer, for anyone thinking about joining Toastmasters, there is a high probability you will be volunteered to participate during the meeting segment called Table Topics. Table Topics is the impromptu curriculum of Toastmasters where a theme or topic captures the essence of questions asked of participants—aka, guests—in a period of one or two minutes.

If you want to feel like you have lived forever, then attend a meeting and participate in Table Topics. A minute with your own thoughts, a microphone, and fifty pairs of eyes on you will wake anyone up.

I remember my first Toastmasters meeting. It was with Voces Latinas, Club #3046, a diverse group dedicated to supporting and developing beginning and advanced speakers with prepared speeches, impromptu speaking, and an evaluation to apply feedback for future speeches. The first question presented to me was, "When life gives you lemons, how do you make the day better?" I loved citrus, and I explained I would plant lemon trees everywhere because it reminded me of Latino culture. A majority of us probably associate lemon trees with Headquarters. My response could have been more colorful, but I was happy to just have words to say.

Answering this first question had me hooked because of how innovative I was forced to be. Most responses would default to making lemonade, but how about a great shortbread lemon tart, which I'd find at a local bakery, and then use the sliced lemon to enhance the already delicious tart?

The Table Topics segment was my favorite because of the uncertainty. This was also the most useful when applied to our daily lives. I found that was the secret and thrill the STEM professionals I admired were making excellent use of. Dale Carnegie once said, "There are always three speeches for every one you actually gave. The one you practiced, the one you gave, and the one you wish you gave." At Toastmasters, I learned to value this and make excellent use of the time I had in any public speaking segment. To this day, this has evolved into a mantra.

Returning to meetings to participate was most natural, and I eventually found myself competing in Table Topics competitions. I made it all the way to the district-level competition.

Now, I have been many things in my lifetime, but a world champion has not been one of them. "As the world champion of public speaking, what's next?" read the contest mediator for the District 52 Table Topics competition at the Castaway in Burbank, California. Dananjaya Hettiarachchi, 2014 Toastmaster world champion of public speaking, was in the audience, as well as one hundred fifty other Toastmasters.

Answering the contest question was difficult. The impostor syndrome kicked in and tested my public speaking abilities. Normally, I was prepared for that sort of thing, but today was different.

Impromptu speaking, which is often recognized as speaking off the cuff, was something I enjoyed very much. Scripts, although important, were not my favorite. Bullet points and outlining major ideas were my second favorite because it allowed for genuine displays of emotion. I recognized my talent, but I also needed to be more organized and intentional with my practice to grow.

I could see my impostor syndrome making its way toward the stage to join me and whisper in my ear, "You have never been a world champion, so how would you know?" The first ten seconds were silent. Usually, this was a technique I would use to ponder, build anticipation, and begin with some powerful and booming anecdote. However, I felt like my spirit and soul jumped out of my body and left me there.

The words I uttered made no sense. My response began with refining my practice as a Toastmaster and continuing to challenge my mind, body, and soul with a magnanimous event like climbing Mt. Everest. There was one audience member who had actually climbed Mt. Everest, and I remember him jumping out of his seat in excitement. As soon as I began speaking about my journey up Mt. Everest, my two minutes were up, and I escorted myself off the stage to the audience's applause—head down, of course.

Leaving the stage, I knew there was no way I had qualified for a place in the top three. Sure enough, I did not qualify, but I left with an epic experience I would not have experienced elsewhere.

Up until that event, I had a little under a year of formal Toastmasters experience, and for someone who was beginning his Toastmaster journey, I came a long way. Although I did not place in the top three, I did make it to the competition that placed me in front of one hundred and fifty other Toastmasters, plus the 2014 world champion of public speaking.

I did not give impostor syndrome the permission to take this achievement and memory away from me. I was critical of my performance for about two minutes, and I never held a grudge with myself for not having a better response.

My response on stage was as good as it could have been at that moment, and I was proud of twenty-three-year-old Bartholomew for making it to that stage.

If I was ever presented with that question again, my answer would look a little like this:

"Well, Topics Master, Toastmasters, and honored guests, as world champion, I would wake up at six o'clock in the morning like any other day. Except for this day, I would stay in bed for an extra four minutes to reflect on the version of Bartholomew who was too afraid to speak."

"You see, speaking was not always a natural skill. Once upon a time, Bartholomew would drip sweat when boarding a bus because of how nervous he would get standing in a crowded place with strangers. He was scared to be seen. He was scared to be judged. He was scared to accidentally offend anyone. When called upon to speak in class, his voice would crack before he uttered a word. And... no, this was not puberty, he was just scared."

"In the classroom, where there was air conditioning, he would drip sweat and make wrinkles on his textbooks that reminded him of his anxiety. When he would return the books, and the clerk asked what happened, his stories would begin with the word 'anxiety.'"

"Talking to the mailman, the liquor store clerk, or the teacher would all make him nervous. Talking to girls was a definite 'no.'"

"All this is true in some parallel version of our universe, and it is important to recognize although it was not my reality today, it is and can be someone else's."

"As world champion, I would continue to develop others the way others have developed me. By lifting others as we rise, we can live in a more thriving and prosperous society. Being a champion means a continued responsibility to develop others and serve as a role model. My greatest role models were the STEM professionals I met after graduating from undergraduate, which inspired me to become a member of Toastmasters International. Thank you."

It's easy to say, "I wish I would have said this." Yet, I find it more satisfying to permanently leave it right here. I am proud of you, Bartholomew.

CHAPTER 13.8

CODE-SWITCHING

Navigating through different worlds is a superpower
It's the gateway from extremely casual to extremely
professional

It shows in greetings, body language, and attire
Navigating through different worlds has no limit

Behaving a certain way is an expectation
You either play the game or sit on the sidelines

I like to play

"Why are you acting so white?" my friends would ask me. This happened right after delivering a presentation on Dorothea Dix, a superintendent of army nurses during the Civil War, for our US History class in seventh grade at Le Conte Middle School. Having grown up in a dominantly Latino community, the norm was Spanglish, a strong use of slang and a certain swagger in the way we switched between English and Spanish while speaking. I, however, spoke in complete sentences and enunciated my words, using proper grammar and sentence structure. So, to be "white" in this context really meant, "Why are you trying to get ahead?"

What did that even mean? The experience of "acting white" was the first time I really noticed this thing formally recognized as code-switching. Simply put, code-switching is being able to adapt language, attire, and culture to the present setting. Code-switching can sound a lot like an actor playing a role in a movie scene, except our different parts of the self are permanent. My vernacular, mannerisms, and nonverbal cues have a wide spectrum from very informal—reserved for my closest friends and family—and extremely formal—reserved for the workplace and business settings. We all do this!

You can take the kid out of the hood, but not the hood out of the kid. It felt as if our thoughts tried to keep us in the hood. This was like growing up in a bucket full of crabs, trying to pull one another down. The biggest problem was not being able to see that was what we were subconsciously doing.

Growing up is probably the most difficult thing anywhere, irrespective of gender, sex, religion, race, ethnicity, etc. Being a child is tough because we will often succumb to social pressures and expectations from our peers. I was no different in those early years.

Once I realized I did not have to completely fit a profile to belong to any one group. I was able to enjoy the benefits of belonging to any group. I associated with the rockers, the loners, the skaters, the nerds, the athletes, the outcasts, and the scene kids. In middle school and high school, these social groups were very important because they meant social mobility. I belonged somewhere and nowhere at the same time.

Trying to fit in became less important the older I got. Learning the customs, behaviors, and languages of the different groups I belonged to became more essential. Adapting meant access to events, other people in the network, and visibility to opportunity and information.

Making new acquaintances became easier because there was plenty to talk about and empathize with. At the same time, I realized there was no obligation to stay in any one group. How? Well, there is something to be said about becoming an ally. An ally is associated with a group for a common purpose. This can be defined by an interest in things like sports, politics, school subjects, music, hobbies, art, dance, theater, travel, and the list goes on.

I did not know it then, but I was up to something by associating with all these groups. Never did I present a front or facade to be like anybody else. I was naturally very interested in many things and people. Collectively, all these interests and people would help define a more authentic sense of self. I was definitely a loner, but never a phony.

This had to be the equivalent of unlocking membership to some fancy country club in Rancho Palos Verdes, CA. Eventually, I realized this was not a skill that was actively taught, but it manifested the more I was exposed to different groups. Code-switching became the outcome.

Code-switching does not mean we have no sense of identity. On the contrary, we can manifest many identities, whether we know it or not. At the root of code-switching, for me, was survival. I enjoyed all the social groups I belonged to for different reasons and learned to enjoy my time with them for different reasons.

My favorite, and one of the most famous public examples, is past president Barack Obama's meet-and-greets. Key and Peele, two Comedy Central sensations, created a skit where after a public announcement, Barack greets guests and switches from "the homie handshake" to a regular hand-shake depending on the demographic before him—black or white. In the skit, he would jump between phrases like "Nice to meet you" to "Come on. What's up, fam? How you doin'? Never forget about that 'cause that's all we got." Finally, the big distinction of all came when Secret Service whispered into Barack's ear, " One-eighth black." Barack responds, "Good afternoon, my octaroon. Come on, bring it in there. Tuck that" (Comedy Central, 2014).

Yes, this was a parody, a direct result of several public instances where President Obama made a display of code-switching during his public appearances. This is a real example many of us persons of color climbing the socioeconomic ladder are familiar with. Just like President Obama, different situations call for different parts of our character to take center stage.

When I am in my engineering setting, there is no way I would speak in my street vernacular as if I were walking in my hometown of Little Armenia. My greetings change from the less formal "Yooo... what's good?" to the more formal "Hey! How are you?"

"Yooo... what's good?" feels most warm. Although it feels like home, it is definitely not considered professional. As a litmus, if you asked me how I greet most people in my mind, it varies depending on the situation.

To illustrate this, I'd like to use two real, familiar examples of what this looks like between being in my neighborhood and a corporate setting.

HOME

"Yooo, what's good, breh?" I greeted my friend on Wilton and Santa Monica, leaning in for a homie handshake and hug with a finger snap at the end.

"Yooo, baby boy! Chillin'. You know, tryin' to make these moves. What's good witchu?" they would say.

"Ayyee, mos def'! I feel it. There ain't no going back. We gots opportunity now. Been grindin' it out and making sure to visit *la jefecita*. She worries sometimes. Too much, but she gets it. Her son is out here trying to get that cheese, bread, and dough."

"My moms trips, too, if I don't at least call to let her know I'm good. I can feel *la chancla* in a text message when I don't. *Jefecitas*, man!"

"Ferreals, though! We owe it to them for us making it this far. I'll catch you later. I gotta meet my bro at the pad."

We lean in for a homie handshake with a hug and a finger snap at the end and part ways.

CORPORATE

"Hey, how are you?" I greeted a colleague in the office with a formal handshake, no hug and no finger snap.

"I am doing well, thank you! Did you see the news on the vaccine? About time!" they would say.

"About time is right! What a supply chain, logistics, and engineering catastrophe! I just hope it works."

"Likewise! I have to run for a meeting two buildings over. I'll see you later. Have a great day."

We part ways with no hug or finger snap.

CODE-SWITCHING TODAY

Code-switching is a part of my DNA. It isn't meant to be malicious or deceitful in any way. It's a complex mechanism we first-generation, people of color, protected groups, LGBTQ, and various nonmainstream groups use to avoid stereotypes. Code-switching is meant for us to display and promote shared interests with the majority and express our own personal leadership aspirations.

Again, it's a mechanism for survival.

One glance at me and you know I am Indigenous, and I am very much proud of this. According to 23andMe, I am 92.5 percent Native American with origins tracing to Central America. One look at me and you can see *el nopal en la frente*. The literal translation is *cactus on his face*, which then translates to having pronounced Indigenous features that cacti can start growing out of his face on top of those already there. Both my parents are of Oaxacan heritage and were born deep in the mountains where you have to make a journey to reach the *pueblos*. My features are strong, I have dark skin, and I definitely stand out.

Growing up, prejudice, rejection, and aggression because of my pronounced features and skin color was normal. I thought of these experiences as a rite of passage every first-generation Mexican experienced. This behavior was normalized. All I could do was adapt and prevent any harm that came to me.

The most dangerous predicament I ever found myself in was during my undergraduate at a hookah lounge while away for a collegiate salsa congress in San Luis Obispo. It was a fun night full of great music, good vibes, and endless dancing. This was the weekend our competition dance team was preparing to perform, and I was an understudy to try to make the team the following year.

I remember having to break from the group to use the restroom. The stalls were all occupied and shut. One of the doors broke open after knocking, and the person in the stall said it was busy. I apologized and stepped away to wait my turn.

After waiting, three white males entered the bathroom and spoke to the guy using the stall that they were here. As they spoke, they formed a triangle around me. I could tell from their body language and facial expressions they were in there to hurt me.

I'd been in this situation in my hood before, but never in a public bathroom. The guy in the stall finished and joined them to form an oddly shaped rectangle.

I will never forget what they said to me.

"This Mexican beaner needs to go real bad," said the white male from the stall.

I was silent, knowing that was true. I had to go.

"Bubba, make sure the stalls are no good." Bubba proceeded to make the stalls inoperable by clogging them until they flooded.

The door opened, and another white male walked in and moved past us, saying, "Excuse me." He proceeded directly to the sink to wash his hands, completely oblivious to the tension in the room.

I made sure to step out before he did, so I was in his line of sight. Without knowing it, that guy saved me. No harm came to me, and I was shaken for the rest of the night. This messed up my night because I could feel that very same group watching me the entire night—like vultures.

I knew if I fed into their perception as the targeted Mexican beaner while in the bathroom, the situation could have escalated immediately. Feeding their aggression would not have been any better. Code-switching kept me out of harm's way by remaining calm and realizing I did not have to throw hands to flee the situation as soon as the last white male walked in to wash his hands.

This kind of aggression happens, and for most of us who are dark, it probably will happen more often. Most of us will not speak about it because it can be embarrassing. I have been conditioned to expect this behavior. As aggressive as that situation was, it did not bother me. The situations that actually hurt are the times I let my guard down in events like social salsa dancing.

I love salsa dancing, and before the COVID-19 pandemic, this was my go-to to meet new people and disconnect from my responsibilities. When I arrive in a new city, this is my go-to activity. Two of my favorite places to go to in Los Angeles are La Granada LA in Alhambra and Steven's Steak & Seafood House in Commerce.

Both locations draw diverse crowds of Asian, European, Latin American, and African people. I loved that! At the same time, the crowd also included all income levels, low socioeconomic through affluent members of society. As diverse as the setting was, I could count on at least one incident of racism from a light-skinned Latina.

"Hi there, I'd love to have the next salsa dance with you. I know you don't want to sit around all night long. Let's share this next song," I said to a woman at Steven's Steak & Seafood House as she sat at one of the dinner booths looking at the dance crowd, waiting to be asked to dance.

"You are Mexican," she responded as if I asked her what my background was.

"Yes, I am."

"Mexicans can't dance."

"Sure we can. Everybody can dance. Dance is just elegant movement."

"No, dark Mexicans can't dance. You *indios* have no rhythm."

"That is a bold statement. Sorry you feel that way."

"I don't think you belong here."

This experience taught me there are some aspects of my appearance I could control to make me appear less like me. That night, I was dressed comfortably in a T-Shirt, skinny jeans, and sneakers. Whenever I defaulted to this outfit, the rejection based on color became a very common incident. When I'd dress up in a coat, button-up shirt, slacks, and dress shoes, this rarely happened. My theory was my attire gave a different impression to bypass the stigma of being dark.

First impressions are important, and I made an extension of myself with the way I dressed. I felt good dressing up, but there were days I wanted to be comfortable. I'd reserve this comfort for my home, where my cats wouldn't judge me based on what I looked like.

Playing this role of higher status was easy because I believe it, but it's exhausting to stay alert all the time.

These occurrences extend into the workplace. They are less obvious, but when you are one of a kind, you notice the subliminal messages. Sometimes those with authority will not have a filter. Two obvious examples of direct targeting were:

- "Gosh, you are so dark."
- "Where I come from, people like you usually get hurt."

There was one particular conversation I remember very well where I was the subject of conversation and trying to be waspy. The remark was very open and direct.

"He tried to dress waspy to fit in, but he won't."

Waspy was a term I had never heard before. Naturally, I consulted Google.

WASP is an acronym referring to White, Anglo-Saxon Protestants with high social status and a disproportional amount of political power and wealth, none of which I fit, but that was the impression I gave.

I love dressing up, and I will, in most social settings, default to dressing up. Subconsciously, I've probably manifested this as a powerplay to assert my legitimacy for having a seat at the table. There is also the leadership component, where leaders are typically dressed the part. One does not need to dress the part, but the audience will usually respond differently because of what we wear and how we behave.

Code-switching is a superpower, and most of us first-generation persons of color will realize embracing code-switching is a sign of leadership. There are perks to it.

In my real estate practice, I've found my white colleagues *wished* they spoke Spanish because of the larger pool of prospects. Spanish is a flex. Embrace it.

Ever notice whether you can switch between being a leader and a follower? That is also code-switching. I learned I do not always have to be a leader, and that is okay. Sometimes, I have to simply be a follower and contributor to display my leadership. It's all a part of the game.

STAGE FOUR

I'M UP TO SOMETHING

CHAPTER 14

BARTHOLOMEW

———

A name is more than your identity
A name is an introduction,
Your first impression

A name is a teammate,
Providing support

A name will follow you everywhere,
The one constant you can rely on

A name can be your voice,
Telling the story of your life

———

My name is Bartholomew. I was born Michael Perez and had no say in my name. Growing up, it was frustrating knowing there were other Michael Perez's in our school. This followed me into university and the workplace.

I wanted my name to be different and make an immediate impression. My name should have the ability to stand-alone just as a building can. Researching Oaxaca helped me discover San Bartolomé Quialana.

Some of the greatest people in history were named Michael:

- Michael Jackson
- Michael Jordan
- Michael B. Jordan

Since 1942, the name Michael has remained in the top fifteen names given in the United States (Behind the name, 2021). It was great to belong to this group of people named Michael, but the longer I lived, the more I wanted to make my own impression.

Being born Michael meant at least one other kid in class, a teen in Physical Ed, and an adult at work was named Michael.

Whenever the name Michael was uttered and Michael and I were in the same room, we would both perk up our ears, raise our heads, and break our necks to respond only to find it was directed at the other Michael. Being the "other Michael" made me doubt if I had my own identity. While I was okay with sharing my name, I was not okay with feeling like the "other Michael."

For brief moments in time, I lived the life of the "other" Michael Perez.

One time in elementary school, I was mistakenly summoned to the nurse's office to provide medical records for some vaccination I never knew I needed but had committed to providing a week ago. In middle school, I was mistakenly summoned to the dean's office to answer to mischievous activities I took no part in—tagging, fighting, and damaging school property—to face the verdict of detention or suspension. In high school, I was mistakenly summoned to meet a counselor on several occasions to test my cognition and storytelling ability as part of some special education assessment. Each time this happened, I was determined not to be the Michael Perez they needed. Although I was relieved not to be any of these Michael Perez's, I felt like my identity was somehow taken away every single time.

When birthdays were involved to verify if I was who I was supposed to be, I was given my identity back. The most exciting part about being mistaken for someone else was trying to figure out what I was being summoned for this time. This felt like being asked to participate on *Jeopardy!* only to be told we had the wrong person with the same name.

Nicknames I earned were great because, at least then, I felt they were unique to me. I was Little Michael to tell me apart from Big Michael, or Rocker Michael because I loved metal music and spiked my hair like I was ready to be featured on a Slipknot music video, which was different from Hip-Hop Michael. There was also the nickname "Tight Space" because of my commitment to skinny jeans, which was different from just being Michael in every possible way.

Growing up, I thought one day I could change my name to something I wanted. While I had no idea how to do it, I knew married people were able to change their name, so maybe I could do something about my own. Marriage was not in my timeline at age twenty-five, but the idea of changing my name had been on my mind since my early teens.

Giving meaning to my name meant I could explore my Oaxacan culture to identify a name that meant something more.

For as long as I could remember, I wanted to visit Oaxaca, Mexico, because that was my parents' Headquarters. Making my own pilgrimage to Oaxaca meant connecting with my ancestors. Friends and acquaintances found it curious both my parents were from there, and yet I knew little to nothing about Oaxaca. Not knowing about my heritage made me feel lost and incomplete, like a puzzle with all the corner and edge pieces but no centerpieces.

I envied my friends who knew of their parents' homelands and their commitment to visiting regularly. My parents' citizenship and financial situation was the largest obstacle for any form of travel growing up. As an adult, I have the privilege to travel.

Making a decent wage afforded me the opportunity to embark on my own pilgrimage, though my obstacle of not having money evolved into the excuse of not having time. There was always something, and it started to feel like self-sabotage by denying myself the opportunity to travel. I was frustrated with myself for not acting and questioned my commitment to connecting with my heritage.

This changed when I decided to book a nonrefundable roundtrip flight to Oaxaca at the end of December 2018. There was no way I was going to let my hard-earned six hundred dollars go to waste.

Going to Oaxaca was important, and it showed in my Google searches.

- *What is the history of the people of Oaxaca?*
- *Who are some of the most famous Oaxacan's in Mexico?*
- *Who are some of the most famous Oaxacan's in the United States?*
- *Are there any Mexican presidents who were of Oaxacan descent?*
- *What are some of the most famous Oaxacan practices and festivals?*
- *How many people live in Oaxaca?*
- *In what city of California do Oaxacan's have a strong community presence?*
- *What industry drives the Oaxacan economy?*

Even better than Google was interviewing my parents before I left. I built expectations based off the memories of their villages and the cities they grew up in. Google Maps could not capture what my parents told me about the coffee fields they harvested, the fresh scent of the mountain and valley air, their favorite restaurants, and taking a trip to el Árbol del Tule, nicknamed the "Tree of Life" because of the images of animals visible in the tree's trunk.

Both my parents' homes were in villages deep in the mountains surrounding the city of Oaxaca. Getting there meant we would have to make a reservation on a shuttle to make sure we had a place for the route the following day. I found these people earned their living by providing this shuttle service. These villages experienced very little development in the infrastructure of their roads, residential buildings, commercial buildings, and public spaces. Yes, they had electricity and running water, but there was definitely no Wi-Fi.

The most common feature of the different villages and cities was they were largely named after saints, which was no surprise because of the large Spanish and Catholic influence on Mexico. That is how I discovered the town of San Bartolomé Quialana in the Southwest region of Tlacolula de Matamoros.

My connection to Tlacolula de Matamoros was from my parents' stories, where they would often travel to visit friends and family, engage in trading and bartering, and gather supplies for their households. It was also in Tlacolula de Matamoros my mother made her attempt at business by selling office and school supplies. This venture was short-lived because she worked on a credit system with her customers, and most of the time, these customers were unable to pay back their debts. Empathy to the struggles of growing up and living in Oaxaca forced my mother to move on from this business practice.

Learning my mother engaged in a short business practice made me proud because it was as if practicing business was in my blood. My connection to Tlacolula de Matamoros was greatly reinforced as a symbol of entrepreneurship that began with my mom's attempt.

Hearing her say she was no good for business because of her sympathy was a learning outcome for me to be mindful of how I made a distinction between logic and feelings. This occurrence was not much different from my eight-year-old experience selling Pokémon cards on my elementary school playground, only to have them stolen after trusting a friend.

I come from several generations of Oaxacan's harvesting coffee for a livelihood. My irrational craving and attraction to a freshly brewed cup of coffee made sense. We always had coffee and pan dulce in our Headquarters. My parents grew up on coffee, which was why we were not too young to start drinking coffee.

Harvesting coffee is an art. My parents and their parents would plant, harvest, process, dry, mill, roast, ground, package, and sell coffee by the pound in Tlacolula de Matamoros. This was how my grandpa paid for my mom's education in the hopes she could lead a life away from the fields. I loved that my family played a role in the world's appreciation for a cup of coffee as their drink of choice.

In October 2018, my last remaining grandfather experienced a brain hemorrhage that almost ended his life. Surviving meant he could no longer cultivate coffee from his lands because of his new dependence on a cane and wheelchair. These sorts of complications were ongoing for three years between strokes and seizures, but he was too stubborn to let the hemorrhage take him to the next world.

Although I have no recollection, I met my grandpa when I was six years old. The only vivid memory from that time was being chased by turkeys after hurling small rocks and taunting them. I absolutely deserved that. Our trip to Mexico was for my parents to figure out what they were going to do about their real estate. The plots of land were largely dedicated to harvesting coffee with enough square footage to build a home.

Oaxacan culture and customs were not a big part of my childhood, with the exception of food. I knew about clayudas, a large, thin, crunchy tortilla covered with beans, cabbage, avocado, chorizo, quesillo (Oaxacan cheese), and salsa. On the rare occasions, we went to La Guelaguetza, an Oaxacan restaurant in Los Angeles, and we would indulge in clayudas and several types of mole.

Then there was the Zapotec dialect, which I never formally learned but understood by context when I was in trouble, or it was time to leave from my cousins' home. Both of my parents knew different dialects of Zapotec, as did a majority of my family who came to the United States. To know I did not retain any of the language despite being around it growing up makes me sad. This was about as much culture as I had growing up.

My siblings and I were far more assimilated to American culture. Assimilating made sense. My parents didn't want us to face the struggles they did by not knowing the language or customs or having the opportunity for an education. Assimilating meant we had a fighting chance of navigating society and advancing from our low socioeconomic status. From this, I gathered further purpose in making sure I had a say in who I was going to be.

My story begins in Oaxaca and only continues to develop in the United States. I committed myself to the dreams and accomplishments unknown to my parents. Up to the moment my mom began her business in Tlacolula de Matamoros, she had done everything she was supposed to, and up until I finished my undergraduate education, I had done everything I was supposed to.

San Bartolomé Quialana translates to "Saint Bartholomew's Sun Rock" because of the black rocks in the valleys surrounding the village. This is a small town where a large part of the rural population goes to trade. A strong impression was made from the name Bartolomé. I've heard the name before on television but had never met anyone named Bartholomew. I liked how the Spanish and English derivatives of the name made a strong impression out loud and on paper.

Bartholomew. Bartolomé. This was the effect I was looking for.

When I first used the name at a Starbucks, the barista taking my order did not believe me and called me out. After I pulled out my business card, the smirk on his face changed, and he proceeded to make my order complimentary. What a great day to be Bartholomew and not Michael.

CHAPTER 15

REAL ESTATE

———

For seventeen years,
Three hundred fifty square feet was Headquarters to six
of us.

I wanted to call the space my "Headquarters,"
I yearned for a space of my own.

I learned to make space for myself.
I learned how to represent the environment that raised me.

———

As a child, I dreamed about all the great things I could buy
after earning my own money: a new house and car, a dog, the
latest video games, and all the chicken nuggets I wanted. The
excitement from selling Pokémon cards at age eight gave me
a glimpse of possibility and the confidence unlimited chicken
nuggets were not out of reach. Business and sales were a part
of my childhood, and I was not going to let that slip away the
same way my cards did. Technically, I handed my collection
to a "friend" who never returned it, which turned out to be
the greatest business lesson: don't voluntarily give away your
goods or services.

Ounces of possibility grew into pounds of reality. I had no conceptual model of volatility, uncertainty, complexity, or ambiguity. When I sold my Pokémon cards, I was solving my problem of high inventory and a demand for cards the other kids were looking for. The most important question I solved for myself was how I could have more customers be interested in what I was offering. The most brilliant idea came while I was collecting Yu-Gi-Oh! cards.

Like Pokémon cards, collecting Yu-Gi-Oh! cards resulted in several repeated cards I did not want or need. When I bought new booster packs, I carefully opened the packaging, so I was able to reseal and sell them. I disclosed to the kids buying them they were opened and repackaged, and all boosters contained a rare of some kind. I only included the rare cards I had multiple copies of. The kids loved it because it was at a discounted price from the card shops, and I loved it because I got rid of inventory.

These early experiences were relevant to explore business and position how I would structure my own adult business practices. As a child, I learned business was about solving problems, whether they be my own or someone else's. My basis of inspiration for business came from a source outside myself: my mom.

Fundamentally, I understood my mother was a housekeeper because rich people with big homes could not clean it on their own since, in my mind, they were busy making money. My mom solved their problem by providing a cleaning service. My mom was a business person without knowing it because she offered a service to solve someone else's problem.

To my mom, this was just a job, but I could see she was running a business of her own. It was this cleaning business that would motivate me to pursue all of my business interests.

Cleaning was important, but my mother reminded us she did not want us to clean toilets for a living. I listened and channeled my energy into my studies. The connection between cleaning those large homes in Beverly Hills, Santa Monica, and West Hollywood was how I wondered more about those houses. The ideas of a house and Headquarters would eventually evolve into seeing them for what they were: real estate.

The only connection I had to owning real estate was yearning to live in a Headquarters of my own. Of course, I dreamed about this as a consumer but never as a real estate professional. The consideration of being a real estate professional never crossed my mind until I thought about owning a home or investing.

In mid-2017, I moved to Lancaster, CA, an hour north of Hollywood, CA, for a new engineering job at a large defense company. This relocation meant I unlocked the possibility of homeownership because housing in Lancaster was much more affordable compared to the inner city of Los Angeles. Homes were about half the price and double the square footage.

Like most first-time buyers, I went through Zillow and Realtor.com to browse homes and favorite the pretty houses my make-believe dog, Alice, and I would enjoy living in. A combination of one-story/two-story, ranch-style, contemporary, and modern homes with large lots, fruit trees, pools, and auxiliary dwelling units made my favorites list. As I favorited listings, I realized this was going to be a lot of space for one person. This was an evolution from the three-hundred-fifty-square-foot studio I grew up in. I was mapping out the decor and how rooms were going to be dedicated as an office, an entertainment/guestroom, and my bedroom. Plus, an extra bathroom! All those years of sharing, and I no longer had to wait to shower, groom, or do the do.

I had a hard time believing this was my decision to make, but it was an absolutely exciting privilege.

The more I researched, the more calls I would get from agents adding me as a prospect. Those fancy algorithms on the real estate websites were being put to work. Most agents were respectful and shared great information, but I was beginning to notice some inconsistencies in what they shared.

Sometimes it was inconsistencies on the specifics of an FHA loan versus a conventional loan and what that meant long term for refinancing and use as a rental property. Then it was whether I could use an FHA loan in the future after purchasing and already owning a home. Being an engineer had nothing to do with the number of questions. As a first-time buyer, I wanted to be informed!

I interviewed nine real estate agents before I finally came to a decision on "the one."

What I enjoyed about this particular agent was she was not pushy, disclosed I was entitled to my own services if I wished, and if she did not know an answer, she would simply say, "Let me get back to you." I appreciated her honesty and professionalism until the time to schedule showings finally came.

Weekends worked best for me due to my work schedule, and on a given weekend, I made myself available to look at listings back to back. Having advanced notice was not enough for her, and she would cancel showings because something would come up elsewhere in her office. As a client, this was infuriating, and I asked if she was able to arrange for someone in her office to meet with me instead. She declined, saying it had to be her.

The impression I had of real estate agents was of deception, excuses, and selfishness.

Having gone through nearly a dozen real estate agents made me question how they became licensed in the first place. When I compared my engineering education to the real estate licensing requirements, real estate seemed like a breeze. Six months of studying, passing a state exam, and about twelve hundred dollars to cover course fees, application fees, fingerprinting, and supplemental tools—the entry barrier was very low.

Becoming wealthy was not a prime motive for becoming licensed. It was the lack of service I received as a first-time home buyer. Failing to find the right agent motivated me to become the right agent for myself and others.

The requirements were not nearly as difficult as engineering school, so I paid my fees and began to study. Every day after work, I'd go to the local Barnes & Noble to study, review problems, and take quizzes until I felt ready. I took a course at a local brokerage to network and learn from the instructor. The great thing about having a bachelor's was having a rhythm on how to study.

I overprepared for my state exam, and it showed. On the day of my exam, I made sure to arrive early at the testing center to relax and ease my own tension.

There were about fifty of us in a room, and we were given stations to take the computerized exam. Taking this exam a second time was not an option, and I can't say I was surprised to be the first one finished.

Over-preparing foreshadowed what would become a part of my real estate practice because continued learning is an unwritten requirement. Not having an answer would not be my excuse for a question a client might one day ask me. Also, having more knowledge than the general public was a large part of our statement of work. Engineering prepared me to learn as quickly and efficiently as possible and how to learn from mistakes.

To avoid making a lot of mistakes, I sought mentorship and expert advice.

My real estate career was inspired by the poor service I received looking for my first home. I was frustrated with the mixed information from different agents. When it came to scheduling, I felt my time was not respected and like my agent wasn't working to represent my best interests. This made me wonder, *How many people out there had a similar experience in their home buying process? How many of those people never revisited homeownership after a bad first impression?*

For most of us, real estate will be the largest purchase we make in our lifetimes, and having the best representation is essential. A home is not just a structure. It comes to life with the stories of those who inhabit its square footage. Engagements, birthdays, anniversaries, promotions, graduations, and family reunions are some of the memories made in a home. Homeownership is also a breakthrough for families climbing the socioeconomic ladder.

A realtor should be an extension of this story in building the family legacy transitioning to their next chapter. We are educators, bridges toward opportunity, and advocates for possibilities and the best possible financial outcomes.

For the actual art of real estate, yes, becoming an agent is as easy as passing a state exam and paying fees, but the real work nobody talks about is the networking, prospecting, and personal branding. A strong sphere of influence and brand can determine the level of success an agent can have in their first year. Statistics show "87 percent of new agents fail and quit after their first year" (Ferry, 2014). This was encouraging because it meant I could become part of the 13 percent who can flourish.

Believing I could be successful was all I needed. It seemed irrational given I had a full-time job during the day, but this was a simple obstacle to overcome after I realized a majority of the public use their weekends to see homes. Figuring out my logistics was one aspect, then it was figuring out what office I wanted to be brokered by.

More important than finding the right broker was experiencing the home buying process and becoming a real estate investor myself. Before I decided to become licensed, I talked to a lot of agents to find a home and was not a fan of their answers when they tried to finesse me. I had the great habit of fact-checking everything I was told, and I did not like the inconsistencies between what they said and what Google said. Maybe I was just overly skeptical about salespeople and thought they were trying to finesse me at every step, but I took these as thoughts my future clients may have about me one day.

My plan going into my first purchase was it would be my home in the time I lived in Lancaster, CA, for about one year. Coming from a three-hundred-fifty-square-foot home growing up, I knew I did not need a lot of space. From listening to and watching several rental investment podcasts and videos, I wanted to have a reasonable amount of cash flow after I paid my principal, interest, taxes, HOA dues, insurance, and repairs. My search was fairly quick, and I closed on my first home on Valentine's Day in 2019 after being licensed. The process was exciting because my first closing would continue to future closings of my future clients.

This experience taught me it was important for future clients to have all questions answered as quickly as possible. Putting my clients at ease was essential, and I had the patience and yearning to do it.

Real estate is a profession where an entire team is required to make the process of homeownership possible. Involved parties include, but not limited to:

- Buyers agent
- Listing agent
- Escrow officer
- Lender
- Title officer
- Inspectors
- Transaction coordinators
- Marketing consultants

Making sure there is a group of dependable and performing partners is of the essence. I quickly learned real estate agents have an additional duty to work with the best professionals possible, both ethically and for the sake of good customer service. For me, service meant living through the process myself as a buyer and homeowner. I was not okay with representing someone if I had not been through the same process myself. Engineering taught me processes and systems are essential to iterate for efficient and reputable performance.

As an adult, becoming a business professional added flexibility a W-2 career would not necessarily allow. Although dropping my engineering career completely for real estate seemed like a very attractive idea, it was definitely not the most reasonable. The best decision I made was to pursue both professions concurrently because engineering prepared me for real estate. Before I would ever feel comfortable enough to pursue business, I had to secure a decent cash flow first with a stable W-2.

Presently, this mindset has brought me to seek my Florida real estate license. By 2022, I will be a practicing agent in the state of Florida, looking for my next purchase and helping others do the same. Real estate has opened up the world I navigate and my perception of wealth and mobility. Learning a new market is going to be fun.

It goes to show, with a little imagination and strategy, Headquarters really can be anywhere.

CHAPTER 16

WEALTH

———

I do not have children today
Everything I do is for them

I don't want to have to tell them
Que no hay dinero
Like my parents told me

Information and resources
Will be abundant for them
With the right ideas and mindset

———

Adversity has been my greatest asset, comparable to the S&P 500, where I developed an index of stories propelling me toward future growth. Coming from low socioeconomic status meant I had a dusty blank canvas with broken edges to etch onto. Before leaving my Headquarters, I thought I wanted to be rich; have a big house, all the nicest clothing, and luxury cars; eat at five-star restaurants; and go on regular weekend getaways. But that was only partially correct.

My definition of wealth has evolved into not having to worry about basic necessities and having a bit extra to go on the occasional trip for however long I'd like.

My parents constantly worried about being able to make payments for rent, food, medical expenses, bus passes, groceries, nannies, and supplies. When I left for university, I worried about rent, food, medical expenses, transportation, pumping gas, school supplies, extracurriculars, and books. A majority of these items were essential. However, I did not want to worry about being able to pay for essentials. Not having to worry about any of this and being able to invest my energy elsewhere was how I began to think about financial freedom.

I didn't want to be at a Shell gas station and have to think about how much I could pump and still be able to pay for lunch the next day. I lived this in undergrad and didn't want to be trapped into this matrix.

Earning interest, dividends, and equity into my accounts, as opposed to overdraft fees, sounded so much better. In the LAUSD, there were no financial literacy courses. In my Headquarters, there were no conversations about wealth. Consideration for generational wealth was a new ideology I would later adopt.

The general public's understanding of money is very limited despite having endless sources of good information. In a nutshell, investing, as opposed to saving, earns you a dividend, which is a monthly/quarterly/annually payment for owning shares in a company. Compare this to the fractions of a percent a financial institution may give you for using a savings account. Financial institutions will lend your savings at much higher percentages so they can reap the benefits.

Yes, the subject of money is very taboo, but why? We earn it, use it, spend it, and will continue to work for it until our last days. Even after we pass, our loved ones may be responsible for whatever assets and liabilities we possess. If we pass away without a trust or will, those assets and liabilities will have to pass through probate to figure out who would be the beneficiary or liable party.

I've conditioned myself to live in the present and operate to establish a future for myself. The way I see it, the first-generation has a lot of catching up to do.

Seeing my parents struggle and worry about money was not the life I wanted to lead, nor did they want that for me. "No hay dinero" was what they said when we asked for toys, wanted to eat at a restaurant, go out with friends, or buy something during a school field trip. "No hay dinero" worked because we knew it was true, but it also created the secondary effect of being unable to envision ourselves as the group that can say, "Sí hay dinero."

I deeply admire my parents for being able to provide for three boys on minimum wage jobs. I don't hold any of my parents' decisions on money against them, but I do take ownership of the lessons learned from my own experiences and unawareness of money from my childhood. One concept my parents drilled into us was saving.

My earliest memory of a savings account was in my fifth-grade classroom when Ms. McKiver had a guest speaker talk about money and why saving was important. I vaguely remember the presentation except for the impression the guest speaker left us with. There was a sense of hope, preparedness for the future, and mastery of financial literacy. The speaker pointed out saving was important because as we got older, we would have an accumulated number of expenses for a home, school, vehicles, emergencies, pets, children... the list went on.

Being an adult is expensive.

I remember going home full of hope and excited to tell my mom about why I should have a savings account. By fifth grade, I was familiar with earning money, but not so much saving it. As soon as we had money, my siblings and I would spend our money on food, Pokémon cards, Yu-Gi-Oh! cards, or video games. By having this savings account, I made the argument I would not be able to touch the money, so I could earn interest and watch it grow over time, just as the Wells Fargo representative described.

Neither of my parents had credit cards or a savings account, operating on a strictly cash basis. My father had a debit card for a short time, but afterward, he noticed the regular fees he was charged for and had no idea why. He closed his account after accumulating several fees. My parents' distrust of financial institutions based on their experiences made sense.

My request for a savings account was denied. Since I was a minor, the account required a parent or guardian to be the primary holder and was required to provide a social security number. Neither of my parents had a social security number, which made me ineligible. This did not upset me because I understood being undocumented meant my parents were at a disadvantage. Being undocumented stopped them from thinking beyond their reality and into the near-limitless possibilities afforded from being in the United States.

Every two weeks, the same guest speaker came back to our classroom to have the registered kids make a deposit into their savings account. I watched enviously as they left class to make their deposits. I didn't want their money. I wanted to be a part of that select group putting money into savings. I wanted to save for the future. I wanted to feel like I was preparing myself for adulthood.

The one thing my parents did consider for the future was *terreno*, or vacant land. My parents never talked to us about their investments or retirement plans, but we were listening.

After buying one of the many calling cards available at the store on Western and Santa Monica, they would talk to their relatives in Mexico about their *terrenos* and any ongoing construction. Calls were encrypted in their Zapotec tongue.

Terrenos meant they had somewhere to go when they decided to move back to Mexico. In their words, it gave us a place to stay when we wanted to visit Oaxaca.

Between savings and real estate, these were the two components of wealth I was familiar with. Although the gap to understand tangible and intangible assets was large, my appreciation for unrecognized signs of wealth were developed: education and mindset. Wealth accumulation and generational wealth were, for a long time, denied to us persons of color. Historically, there were laws, practices, and legislation that would not allow the open penetration into a wealthy status.

Today, becoming financially free and remaining informed are blurred subjects but available to those who seek its fruit of labor and ripeness.

Influencers like Graham Stephan, Patrick Bet-David, Robert Kiyosaki, Dave Ramsey, and Brandon Turner taught me about wealth. Well, at least their online personas and literature did. My favorite breakdown of wealth has to be from Patrick Bet-David, who, in his YouTube video titled "Three Steps on How to Be Wealthy," summarized becoming wealthy into three steps:

1. Learning the skills of sales.
2. Choosing an industry.
3. Choosing a group of people to run with.

As an engineer and STEM professional, I loved this formula because it was easy to follow and prioritized where we should invest our energy.

The biggest prerequisite to wealth is believing we are worthy and capable of obtaining wealth.

The different components of becoming wealthy include education, self-awareness, and giving. Education means remaining informed on the subject matters that build wealth; for me, they are real estate, investing, and writing. Self-awareness means I am constantly taking care of my mental health, addressing my traumas and frustrations, and realizing what brings me joy. Giving means remaining engaged with the community to help others develop.

When my future children arrive, I want them to think of their father as a man who stopped at nothing to make his ambitions come true. That despite his adversity as a first-generation Latino born to immigrant parents with a low socio-economic status, he still evolved into success and wealth. This book has little to do with me and everything to do with them, my children. Although there is no certainty they will accept and resonate with my words, anticipating they one day will is reason enough. This must be what every parent feels and thinks when their child leaves home for the first time.

Por fin te entiendo, mamá.

CHAPTER 17

THE ARTS

Arts are more than passion
Art is sharing what words cannot

Stability and flexibility came
Before artistry was appreciated

Writing was my outlet
I had to be okay with imperfection

Once that happened
Filling pages was easy

Engineering perfect sentences was not my interest. Sharing my story about how science, technology, engineering, and mathematics (STEM) influenced my life for greater control, empathy, and sharing of information has been my interest. Art can take many forms, and I chose storytelling. Stories fascinate me because of how old storytelling is. Before googling, there was storytelling.

The earliest stories that remain in existence are paintings on cave walls. Although I was tempted to submit a series of drawings on different pages, I knew putting words together might be of better use. After all, a Google search can sort through my words with their fancy algorithms.

Engineering financed my freedom to pursue several interests, but writing established the greatest feeling of control and relief I have ever felt. The only other instance where I felt this phenomenon of control and relief was going to therapy to deal with the many childhood traumas I pent-up.

Writing is therapy and a luxury. Writing is greater than my desire to own a Porsche, own more real estate, create an impeccable wardrobe, and travel the world.

Figuring out how I want to express myself is the luxury. Why stop at writing when I can also act, sing, and dance to convey emotion? Where do I get my inspiration? YouTube!

- Eva Longoria spoke about the biggest risk she took during an interview for Build Like a Woman YouTube channel. "Moving to Hollywood. I was twenty-one. I just graduated from college and never aspired to be an actress. Literally, one day, I said I wanted to be an actor… I felt this guiding power, and I had twenty-two dollars in my bank account. I knew nobody in LA or ever flew out of Texas" (Build Like a Woman, 2019).
- Eminem was interviewed in 1999 to speak on life as an artist and his success from his *The Marshall Mathers LP.* "Yeah, life is definitely better now. I really don't want it to get much better because then I won't have anything to rap about" (MTV, 2020).

- Hasan Minhaj described how racism hurts immigrants by reaching into his own life. "My dad's from that generation, like a lot of immigrants, where he feels like if you come to this country, you pay the American dream tax. Like, you're gonna endure some racism and if it doesn't cost you your life, well, hey, you lucked out, pay it. There you go, Uncle Sam" (Netflix is a Joke, 2021).

These are some stories that inspire me. I don't always have to understand the experience to appreciate the tenacity required to overcome the seemingly impossible. When I hear these people speak, I feel aligned while looking at them and thinking, "I understand you because you are saying what I feel and know." We have yet to meet, but we are not much different in that we had to overcome adversities to become people we are proud of.

Writing is the second platform I have enjoyed and appreciated for self-expression. The first is dance, and the third is singing. Their order is irrelevant because they all arrived in my life for different reasons and have a purpose in their appropriate settings.

I first found dance in undergraduate. Being tired of standing by in a Latin dance venue, I built the courage to take lessons and join a dance team. My feet, mind, and spirit were happy whenever there was salsa music playing, and I knew what to do at every count. The counts in dance go, o*ne, two, three, five, six, seven,* and in the background, we hear the claves, bongos, timbales, trumpet, piano, and cowbell leading an audience.

All of a sudden, an empty room metamorphosed into a venue of salsa dancers from all over the state, country, and world. Dancers are in their elegant attire on a Friday night at Alhambra where we dance. Smiles, laughter, a gentle gaze of the eyes, fierce shoulder shimmies, and body rolls take over. The beauty of dance is in the body language between two people enjoying the moment. This is what I learned to love.

Singing came into my life after experiencing a rear-end accident that forced me to stop my CrossFit and lifting at Code3 in Hawthorne, CA. This was devastating and forced me to find a less high-impact activity that would not put any strain on my back. The alternative to deadlifting three hundred-plus pounds was singing.

Before this experience, I did not think my vocal cords could pitch-match the keys of the piano. I found the singer's studio *The Voice by Chelsea,* where I met Coach Julia Ragusa as a result of my car accident. With Coach Julia, we explored techniques and a variety of songs from John Legend, Lady Gaga, Shawn Mendes, and Elvis Presley to develop my technique. This was my therapy in lieu of CrossFit.

Through singing, I found I am a baritone or tenor. This is to be confirmed because it has only been three months of lessons. While singing Lady Gaga's "Shallow," I discovered I could feel the words and the feelings Lady Gaga was sharing with her audience. The same effect occurred when exploring John Legend's "All of Me." Without realizing it, I expanded my spectrum of understanding toward the world. Art is full of compassion.

My story is not lesser or greater than any other person's story. My story is just mine. If I am able to have someone say, "He is describing exactly what I have been feeling and going through," then the late nights and early mornings will have been worth it. My goal has been to prepare anyone going into STEM to consider what their future can look like if they want an untraditional lifestyle. At some point, we may have the realization engineering is not enough because we hold so many interests, and that is okay.

Art may not be the most obvious element in STEM, but when we think about design, system engineering, and processes, we suddenly realize the mastery and creativity involved with our craft as engineering professionals. The standard convention in my community is to default to STEM, resulting in the "A" dropping off. STEAM would be a more accurate depiction of what we are trying to convey.

Organizations like the Institute for Arts Integration and STEAM help develop professionals for use of arts-integrated approaches to nurture the unique and personal connection we can cultivate to support our students. Science, technology, engineering, art, and mathematics all intersect very beautifully.

The arts help connect the logical to the illogical and the brain to the heart. Art is an illustration of the experiences, feelings, and resolutions we make as humans.

Next time you are at a loss for words, find an artistic way to express those feelings and join me in the relief, satisfaction, and thrill you experience in the moment.

CHAPTER 18

CLOSING THOUGHTS

———

By the time this is published and out in the world, I will have lived thirty fruitful years on our beautiful rock flying in outer space. On this rock, I've been able to overcome adversity, develop into a multidisciplinary professional, and lead by example for aspiring professionals wanting to have multiple careers concurrently.

When I am interviewed, I regularly visit the idea of Maslow's hierarchy because it perfectly defines the evolution taking care of the basic necessities like food, water, shelter, rest, and security. Taking care of these then allows us to focus more on things like cash flow and creativity.

As a child, I grew up thinking my family had no money and always wondered why we would not move out of our three-hundred-fifty-square-foot apartment. My parents would not talk to us about money, the future, or how we should establish our place in the world. No fault to them, but they had tunnel vision based on their status as undocumented immigrants.

Moving away from home was the first conscious effort to live a life I could be proud of and break from the undocumented immigrant mindset my parents lived.

My decision to leave Headquarters at seventeen was conscious and deliberate toward arriving at self-actualization. Developing my identity allowed me to confront my traumas and build a community of meaningful relationships.

Graduating from CSUN as a mechanical engineer was one of the most important financial investments I made without knowing. The financial security from being an engineer has afforded me peace of mind to pursue my multicareer path.

I hope we, Latinos and the first-generation—yes, this includes white people too—can use education as a tool to move forward, but we should not stop there. Engineering provided me an income I could be proud of and was enough to subsidize my remaining ambitions of real estate, investing, and writing.

If there is anything I would like for you to take away from this book, it's no matter your circumstances, that situation does not have to stay your outcome. You have the power to change direction, but you must take ownership of your own development and see beyond what is present today.

Consider everything you did an hour ago and everything you will do tomorrow. Yup, you are up to something!

ACKNOWLEDGMENTS

———

None of this would have been possible without my early sup-porters! Your eyes passing over these words means the world to me. I love you all. Thank you for being the support system within the support system I needed.

To my parents, Clara and Rene, thank you for doing the best you could to raise me. My cats, April and Aife, thank you for listening whenever I had to read a chapter aloud.

To Professor Koester: thank you for encouraging me to put my story out into the world and helping me get past a terrible first draft.

To the NDP staff: thank you for making this book a reality and working with me every step and leap forward. Thank you, Rebecca Bruckenstein, Michelle Pollak, and Viengsamai Fetters, for keeping me accountable and motivated through the revisions process.

To past professors, teachers, mentors, and coaches who always encouraged me: thank you for seeing something in me. It still means the world today as I develop others.

Deepest gratitude for those who contributed to my Indiegogo campaign:

Adan Velasquez	Aldo Martinez Martinez
Alejandra Montoya	Alex Geronilla
Alex Salazar	Alexandra Arroyo
Alexis Moreno	Allen Raymond Dumaua
Alma Angel	Amanda Montoya
Ammar Mufleh	Amparo Ostojic
Ana Artiaga	Andrea Lopez
Andrew Delgadillo	Angel Hernandez
Angelica Morfin	Arnold Morales
Augusto Rodriguez	Balfred Carrillo Martinez
Benjamin Ruvalcaba Alonso	Bertrand Perdomo-Ucles
Brenda Beltran	Bryan Hernandez
Bryant Garcia	Buck Moore
Carlos Hernandez	Carlos Marin
Carlos Vivas	Carol Naranjo
Christin Young	Christopher Aston
Chrys Koomson	Claudia Navarrete-Castellanos
Crystal De Agueros	Cynthia Gurrola
Dania Barajas	Daniel Valadez
Daniela Caballero	Daniela Solis
Dario Tejeda	Darren Aguilar
David Gaeta	Diana Silveyra
Diego E. Montenegro	Diego Vilchez
Douglas Scherer	Edgar Torres
Eduardo Naranjo	Eduardo Ugalde
Eileen Noriega	Elaine Cope
Elio Morillo	Emily Anne Vargas

Emily Gonzalez

Erika Barrales

Ernesto Suarez

Eugenio Ulloa

Fabiel Nunez

Fernando Gutierrez

Frank Barragan

Gabriel Quihuiz

Gabriela Coe

Gustavo Correa

Helena Magaña

Jaideep Upadhyay

James Chung

Jennifer De Avila

Johanna Quintanilla

Jose Maximiliano Diaz

Joseline Valenzuela

Juan Avila

Juan Flores-Zamora

Juanita B. Gonzalez

Julissa Alejandra Godinez

Karen Abarca

Katherine Cabrejo

Kimberly Coronel

Laura Orellana

Lidia Alfaro

Lisbeth Echeverria

Luis Jarquin

Luis Martinez

Marcos Cruz

Mariel Cisneros

Eric Koester

Erin Hong

Estefania Ochoa

Evelyn Luna

Felipe Arguijo

Francisco Legorreta

Gabriel Luna Bautista

Gabriela Chavez

Guadalupe Menchaca

Heather E. Vanner

Isela Lopez

Jaime Pena

Janet Llopiz Caride

Jesus Ojeda

Jose A. Guzman Jr.

Jose R. Olmedo

Josh Tan

Juan Bahena

Juan Vela

Julio Aguilar

Justin Borreta

Karol Alcaraz

Katrina Petney

Krystal Sims

Leah Miramontes

Linda Cifuentes

Lorena Venegas

Luis Maquial

Marbeya Brown

Maria Lucas

Mariela Robledo Morales

Marina Chavez

Mark Delarosa

Mattia Day

Mayra Tubac

Michael Guiracocha

Miguel Guerrero

Mina Tawfick

naotakurix78

Norma Catalina Soriano

Pedro Jimenez

Rafael Reyes

Reymundo Antonio Rodríguez Jr.

Roberto Morales

Rosa Juarez

Samantha Guzman

Sara Colon

Sarah Al Janabi

Sevanne Calle

Sienna Jackson

Susana Juarez

Thelma Federico

Vanessa Hernandez

Virna Cortez

Mario M. Oropeza

Matthew Gomez

Mayra Gonzalez

Mercedes G. Castillo

Michelle Le

Miguel Larios

Naomi Hernandez Ramirez

Nixon Campos

Omar Rojas

Peter Cortez

Rebecca Martinez

Ricardo Martin

Rolando Caceres

Roy Lara

Samantha Perez

Sara J. Martinez

Sergio Ortiz

Shirley Jean Cruz

Stephanie Fitzsimmons

Tamara Gonzalez

Tony Ibarra-Leyva

Victoria Banuelos

Zoraida Martinez Duarte

APPENDIX

——

INTRODUCTION

Espriu, Laura. "How Latinx experience the Impostor Syndrome" *LinkedIn*. January 30, 2020. https://www.linkedin.com/pulse/how-latinx-experience-impostor-syndrome-laura-espriu/?articleId=6628820102253031424.

Guida, Humberto. "The Future of the American Economy is Latino." *LATV*. October 4, 2020. https://latv.com/the-future-of-the-american-economy-is-latino/

Latino Donor Collaborative. *Fast Facts: Latinos in America*. September 23, 2020. https://www.latinodonorcollaborative.org/.

Salas, Sean. "The $2.6 Trillion US Latino Market: The Largest And Fastest Growing Blindspot Of The American Economy." *Forbes*. September 27, 2020. https://www.forbes.com/sites/seansalas/2020/09/27/the-26-trillion-us-latino-market-the-largest-and-fastest-growing-blindspot-of-the-american-economy/?sh=559c979f9e62.

SALUTATORIAN

Islas, M. Rene. "Equity in Education: Children Who Are Overlooked for Gifted & Talented Education." March 7, 2017. https://edublog.scholastic.com/post/equity-education-children-who-are-overlooked-gifted-talented-education.

Urban Dictionary. s.v. "Salutatorian." By diosmioalejandra. May 18, 2008. https://www.urbandictionary.com/define.php?term=Salutatorian.

DECIDING ON A MAJOR

Adams, Susan. "The College Degrees With The Highest Starting Salaries in 2015." *Forbes*. November 19, 2014. https://www.forbes.com/sites/susanadams/2014/11/19/the-college-degrees-with-the-highest-starting-salaries-in-2015/?sh=2f43275e2403.

Day, Jennifer Cheeseman. "STEM Majors Earned More Than Other STEM Workers." *Census*. June 2, 2021. https://www.census.gov/library/stories/2021/06/does-majoring-in-stem-lead-to-stem-job-after-graduation.html.

REFLECTIONS OF AN UNDERGRAD

Meyer, Lily. "In 'Can't Even,' Burnout Is Seen As A Societal Problem — One We Can't Solve Alone." *NPR*. September 22, 2020 https://www.npr.org/2020/09/22/915590402/in-cant-even-burnout-is-seen-as-a-societal-problem-one-we-cant-solve-alone.

TOASTMASTERS DISTRICT 52 COMPETITION

Ingraham, Christopher. "America's top fears: Public speaking, heights and bugs" *The Washington Post. October 30, 2014.* https://www.washingtonpost.com/news/wonk/wp/2014/10/30/clowns-are-twice-as-scary-to-democrats-as-they-are-to-republicans/.

CODE-SWITCHING

Comedy Central. "Key & Peele - Obama Meet & Greet." September 24, 2014. Video: 1:53. https://www.youtube.com/watch?v=nop-WOC4SRm4.

BARTHOLOMEW

Behind the Name. "Michael." Popularity in The United States. Accessed: October 17, 2021. https://www.behindthename.com/name/michael/top.

REAL ESTATE

Ferry, Tom. "87% of All Agents Fail in Real Estate!" Tom Ferry. December 4, 2014. https://www.tomferry.com/blog/87-of-all-agents-fail-in-real-estate/.

WEALTH

Bet-David, Patrick. "3 Steps on How to Be Wealthy." September 3, 2015. Video: 8:48. https://www.youtube.com/watch?v=-o-oG9ZmEBo.

THE ARTS

Build Like a Woman. "Build Like A Woman: Eva Longoria." November 7, 2019. Video: 23:35. https://www.youtube.com/watch?v=C9yVibbsJBY&t=934s.

MTV. "Eminem in Detroit (1999) | Going Back | MTV News." May 23, 2020. Video: 7:59. https://www.youtube.com/watch?v=Eu-0GicOi4Sk.

Netflix is a Joke. "Hasan Minhaj on How Racism Hurts Immigrants." June 14, 2021. Video: 6:39. https://www.youtube.com/watch?v=P3RyCtbwBDA.